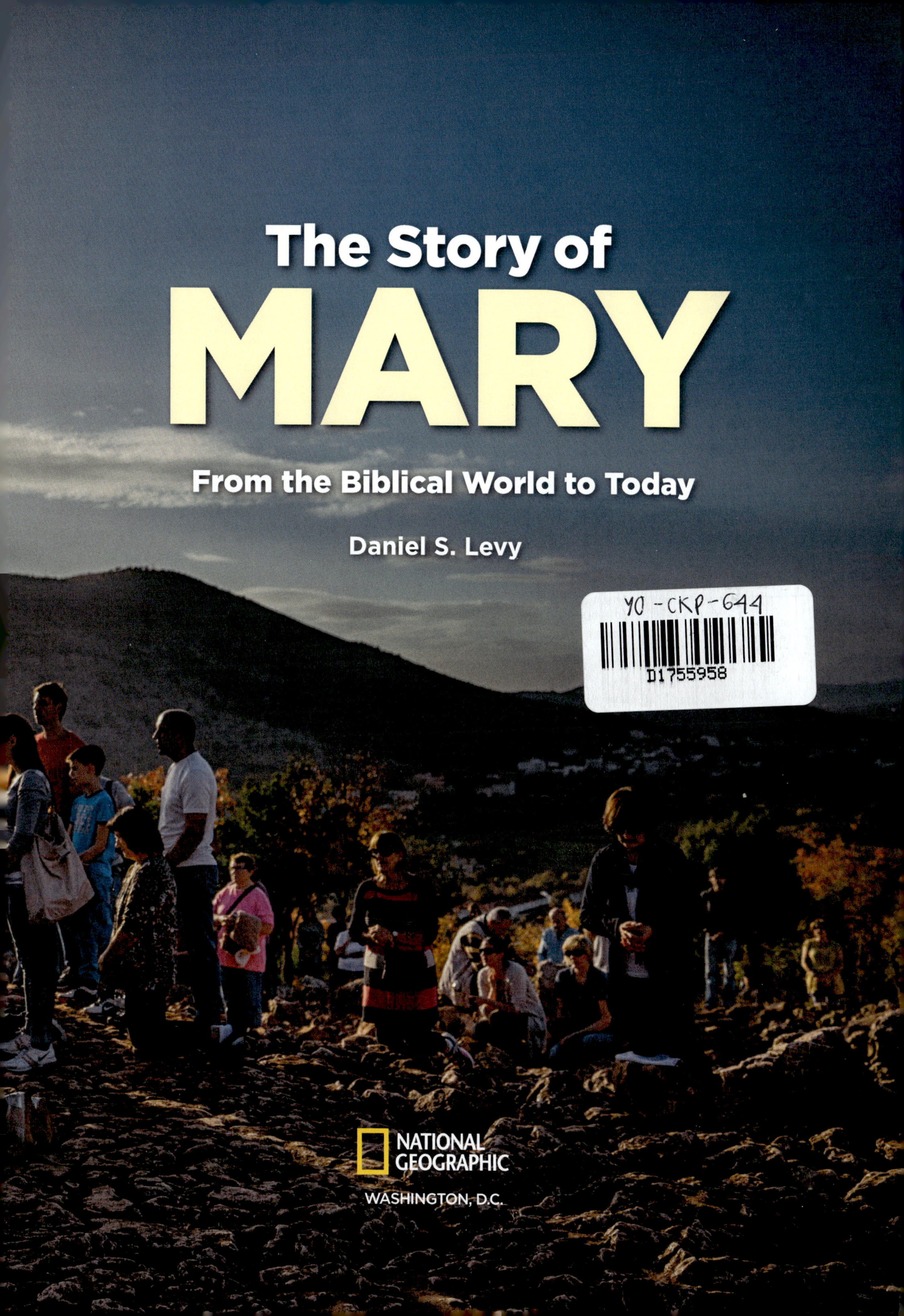

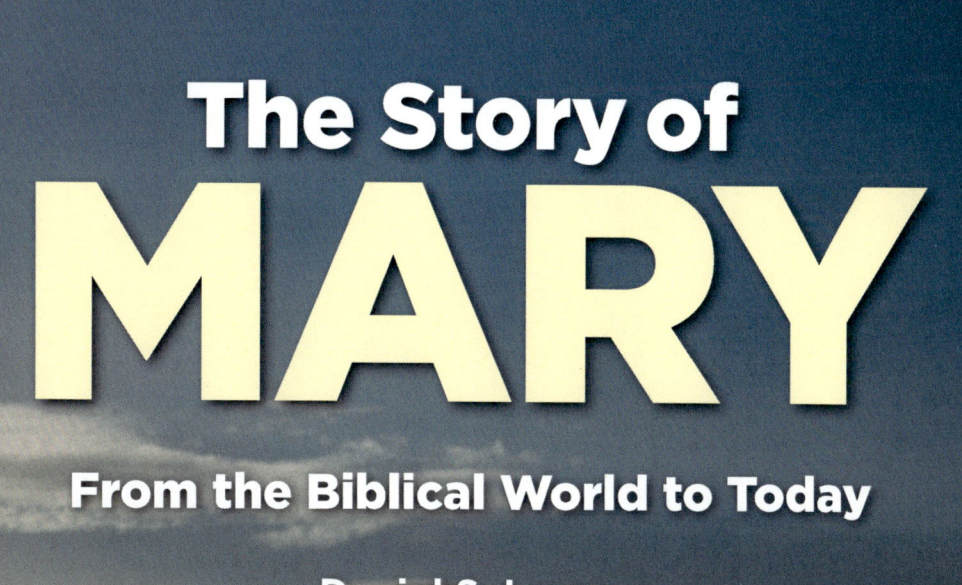

The Story of
MARY

From the Biblical World to Today

Daniel S. Levy

NATIONAL GEOGRAPHIC

WASHINGTON, D.C.

CONTENTS

Introduction 4

CHAPTER 1
HER EARLY LIFE
10

CHAPTER 2
MARY'S TIMES
28

CHAPTER 3
JESUS COMES OF AGE
48

CHAPTER 4
SAINT MARY
70

CHAPTER 5
EVER PRESENT
92

Illustrations Credits 112

COVER: "Madonna and Child" (oil on canvas) by Giovanni Battista Salvi da Sassoferrato (1609–1685), Palazzo Ducale, Urbino, Italy. THIS PAGE: "The Nativity at Night" by Guido Reni, an Italian baroque painter. PREVIOUS PAGES: The faithful flock to Apparition Hill in Medjugorje, Bosnia, where Mary was said to have appeared in 1981.

INTRODUCTION

THE MEANING OF MARY

Mary is one of the most famous women in history, an exemplar of purity. But what do we really know about this young Jewish girl named Miriam who became the mother of Jesus? We meet her at the start of the Gospel According to Luke and learn that "the angel Gabriel was sent from God to . . . a virgin betrothed to a man named Joseph, of the house of David, and the virgin's name was Mary."

When Gabriel arrived, he told her, "Hail, favored one! The Lord is with you" (Luke 1:26-28). He then told Mary what was being asked of her. After that, we have just brief appearances by Mary. We see her visiting Elizabeth, the birth of Jesus, bringing her son to the Temple, the arrival of the Magi, the flight to Egypt, Passover in Jerusalem, Mary at the Wedding in Cana, her efforts to see Jesus during his ministry throughout the Holy Land, her presence at his Crucifixion, and then as she is surrounded by her son's followers after the Resurrection.

That is all that the New Testament tells us of the Mother of God. The books do not tell Mary's story; they are instead about the life, death, and resurrection of Jesus. But as the human who was and still is closest to God and the only person present at all the important stages of his brief presence on Earth, Christians and others have wanted to know more about Jesus' most devoted disciple despite the paucity of solid information on her.

A detail from Michelangelo's "Pietà," where Mary cradles her son following his Crucifixion

HAIL MARY

Mary has been exalted and called by many names. Gabriel bestowed on her the title "Favored One." Since then, she has been called Queen of Heaven, Mother Inviolate, Ark of the Covenant, and Tower of Ivory. People have been petitioning Mary for nearly 2,000 years and reciting the Hail Mary for some 1,000 years:

Hail Mary, full of grace. / The Lord is with thee. / Blessed art thou amongst women, / and blessed is the fruit of thy womb, Jesus. / Holy Mary, Mother of God, / pray for us sinners, / now and at the hour of our death. / Amen.

This is not a prayer but a plea for assistance in seeking God's love. These profound lines are also called the Angelical Salutation. The first part embodies the greeting Gabriel made at the Annunciation. The second is from Mary's visit to Elizabeth and her relative's crying out, "Most blessed are you among women, and blessed is the fruit of your womb" (Luke 1:42). The last plea comes from the Council of Trent, a series of ecumenical meetings held in northern Italy in the 16th century to counter the Protestant Reformation. At one of those gatherings, the line "pray for us sinners, now and at the hour of our death" was approved.

THE FIRST DISCIPLE

Part of the Reformation was in response to what Protestants saw as the idolatry of Mary. But despite their disagreement with her exaltation, there has been a growing acceptance of her prominence within the spiritual lives of many Christians. The rise of feminism in the later 20th century encouraged interest in women in the Bible. And as traditionally Catholic Hispanics joined Protestant denominations, many brought with them their devotion to Mary. As Timothy George, dean of the evangelical Beeson Divinity School, noted, "Mary was a disciple of Christ before she was his mother, for if she had not believed, she would not have conceived."

UNDERSTANDING THE INFINITE

Mary is a reminder of humanity's brief moments on Earth during which we feel joy, warmth, love, and grief over those closest to us. That young girl from Nazareth has helped us understand the infinite. Who is Mary, and why did God choose her? It is a question people have asked for the last 2,000 years, and it is her life and influence that we explore in these pages. ∎

BELOW: **The Angel Gabriel appearing to Mary, and hailing her as the "favored one!"** OPPOSITE: **A boy at the Deir al Adra monastery in Minya, Egypt, reaches for Mary.**

THE STORY OF MARY

Map of Mary sightings

Starting in the 16th century, the Roman Catholic Church instituted a strict vetting process for miracles like the 2,000 sightings of the Virgin Mary claimed since 40 C.E. To be worthy of belief and church support, apparitions must be deemed miraculous with a high degree of certainty and in line with church doctrine, and found to have a positive impact.

SUPERNATURAL
The local bishop or the Vatican finds evidence of the supernatural (the occurrence of a miracle).
- Recognized by the Vatican after approval by local bishop
- Approved by local bishop
† Virgin Mary's appearance to future saint

EXPRESSION OF FAITH
- Visions are approved as worthy of faith expression but are not established as supernatural.

LOCAL TRADITION
- Visions are part of local traditions and saint biographies but are not formally investigated.
† Virgin Mary's appearance to future saint

UNCONFIRMED
- Apparitions are not supernatural, have not yet been investigated, or are under investigation.

Centuries of Miracles

COUNCIL OF TRENT
One of the most important ecumenical councils in Roman Catholic Church history, it defined doctrine and an approval process for visions.

Each vertical segment represents the date of an apparition's first sighting.

| Recognized by the Vatican after approval by local bishop | Approved by local bishop |
| Expression of faith | Local tradition | Unconfirmed |

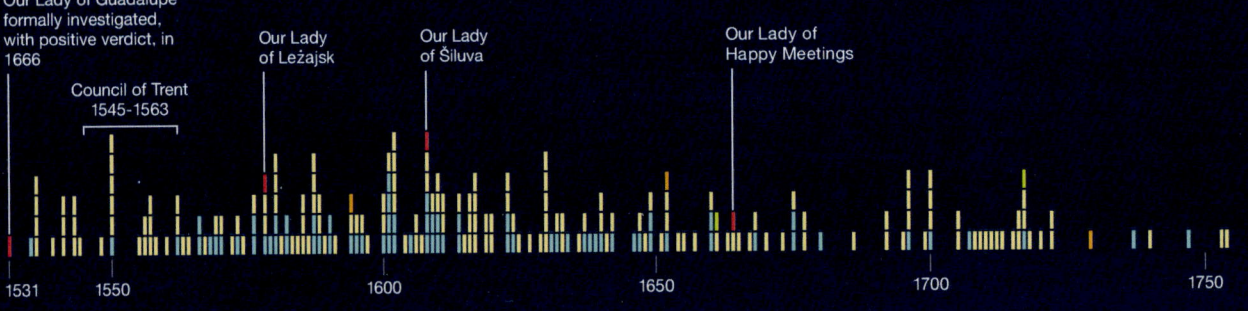

VIRGINIA W. MASON, NGM STAFF; VICTORIA SGARRO
SOURCE: MICHAEL O'NEILL, MIRACLE HUNTER

CHAPTER 1

Her Early Life
JOACHIM AND ANNE'S SPECIAL CHILD

"Can anything good come from Nazareth?" wondered the disciple Nathanael (John 1:46). This sleepy Judean village near the Sea of Galilee sat at the edge of a vast, wealthy Roman empire in a land conquered in 63 B.C.E. by the Roman general Pompey and turned into a client state, with Herod as its king.

While Nazarenes yearned for independence and a return to ancient glory, most Jews like Anne and Joachim focused on closely following the laws set out in the Bible. What little we learn about Mary's parents comes from the Apocrypha volume, the Protoevangelium of James. This second-century work was compiled to help flesh out Mary's childhood and emphasize how miraculous she and her son, Jesus, were. Such a special young woman would have come from pious parents. While Joachim and Anne had a good marriage, this elderly pair yearned for one thing they could not have: a child. Joachim's inability to sire a son or daughter so grieved him that one day, he retreated to the countryside.

There, he pitched a tent and fasted for 40 days and nights and vowed, "I will not go down either for food or for drink until the Lord my God shall look upon me." Anne, meanwhile, said she would "bewail my childlessness." She sat in her garden and lamented, "Alas! Who begot me? And what womb produced me? . . . Because even the earth brings forth its fruits in season." An angel appeared and told her, "The Lord has heard your prayer, and you shall conceive, and shall bring forth; and your seed shall be spoken of in all the world." An angel also came to Joachim, saying that God had heard his prayer.

ABOVE: **Stone vessels like this one were impervious to impurity and guaranteed ritual purity.**
OPPOSITE: **Mary, Joseph, and Jesus fled to Egypt to avoid Herod's murderous wrath.**

THE STORY OF MARY

THE BIRTH OF MARY

When Joachim returned home with his flock, Anne ran out to her husband. She embraced him and told him, "Behold . . . the childless shall conceive." As thanks, Joachim brought "ten she-lambs without spot or blemish" as an offering to the Lord, "twelve tender calves" for the priests and elders, and "a hundred goats for all the people."

This was a special child, one promised by the angels. While conceived like all other humans, this infant would prove to be divinely unique. For as church leaders would much later proclaim, before Anne's pregnancy, the unborn child's soul was shielded from original sin, the stain all bear because Adam disobeyed God when he ate the forbidden fruit, bringing about his and Eve's banishment from the Garden of Eden. Nine months after Joachim returned from the fields, the once-barren Anne went into labor. Her midwife, following the practice of the time, probably rubbed her stomach with olive oil and myrtle, anointed her with herbs and oils, and bathed her. Then, like the once barren Sarah who gave birth to the patriarch Isaac and Hannah who birthed the prophet Samuel, Anne's child arrived. When the midwife told her that she had a little girl, Anne rejoiced, saying, "My soul has been magnified this day."

This first-century C.E. thin-necked earthenware jug was probably used for wine or water.

A BELOVED DAUGHTER

They named her Miriam, the same name as Moses' sister. The child we know as Mary was swaddled and laid on a hay-filled pillow with a channel, similar in shape to a feeding trough, so she could not roll over. Anne and Joachim proved to be attentive parents. According to James in the Protoevangelium, Anne made a sanctuary in her bedchamber for her daughter. When Mary turned one year old, Joachim threw a feast and invited priests, scribes, and elders. Anne said, "I will sing a song to the Lord my God for He has looked upon me . . . and the Lord has given the fruit of His righteousness." On Mary's third birthday, the family headed south to the Temple in Jerusalem. The sight of the structure, the glistening limestone complex that Herod, the king of Judea, had been rebuilding, transfixed

Mary. There the priest blessed and kissed the toddler, saying, "The Lord has magnified your name in all generations." Mary was happy, and when the priest set her down, the small girl danced with joy.

Mary is believed to have been quite beautiful. She would have had Middle Eastern features, with dark hair and eyes, spoken an Aramaic patois, and heard Hebrew, as well as Latin and Greek, around town and in the surrounding area. Modesty was essential for girls and women, and Mary probably wore simple garments, with linen undergarments overlaid with a tunic with long sleeves. Around her waist would be wrapped a girdle, and another one under her bosom. Over her shoulder, Mary draped a cloak that might sport geometric patterns, and when she was outside, a veil covered her hair.

This 15th-century painting depicts Joachim and Anne as they await their special child.

Like other girls at the time, Mary spent her days helping Anne, fetching water as well as assisting with planting and harvesting. She passed much of her time preparing food for meals, as well as for the Sabbath and assorted religious holidays and weddings. Girls rarely received an education, and Mary most likely could not read. But she grew up in a society imbued with an oral tradition. At home as well as in and around Nazareth, Mary would have heard scriptures, stories, and public readings. Thus, from an early age, she would have learned the necessary rituals of Jewish life and would have been able to recite prayers for meals and other occasions. ■

THE STORY OF MARY

THE MOTHER OF JESUS

※

While the Bible is filled with sages like Moses who lived until the age of 120, Noah until 950, and Methuselah until 969, the life expectancy two millennia ago stood closer to 30. Most people did not live past their 15th birthday. As a result, girls married quite early in order both to guarantee their virginity and enable them to bear numerous children.

"There is no luxury called adolescence in that world," notes Byron McCane, a historian at Florida Atlantic University. "As soon as young men and women show that they are capable of reproducing, they get married and start to have children." Families arranged these unions, and it is possible that in such a small place as Nazareth, which had only a few hundred people, Mary would have known Joseph. This local carpenter, who was a descendant of King David, was possibly an older widower.

THE ANNUNCIATION

Mary and Joseph became betrothed, the first part of a two-stage Jewish wedding ceremony. For the initial part, called the *erusin,* Joseph would give a *mohar,* a dowry, to Mary's family. At that point, he and Mary were legally wed. Yet by tradition, while they were married, the wife continued to live with her parents for about a year after the betrothal. During that time, Mary and Joseph would look forward to a *nissuin,* a wedding ceremony, after which she would move out of her parents' home and settle in Joseph's house.

> GABRIEL TOLD THE TEENAGER: "HAIL, FAVORED ONE! THE LORD IS WITH YOU"  (LUKE 1:28). MARY, THE ANGEL SAID, WOULD HAVE A CHILD.

But following the erusin, and as the family planned the wedding celebration, the angel Gabriel appeared to Mary. The Gospel According to Luke tells us that he informed the teenager that she had been chosen by God: "Hail, favored one! The Lord is with you" (Luke 1:28). Mary, the angel said, would have a child. This confused the young woman, who replied, "How can this be, since I have no relations with a man?" Gabriel explained that although she was still a virgin, a transcendent event would occur. "The holy Spirit will come upon you, and the power of the Most High will overshadow you," he said, and "therefore the

Raphael's High Renaissance take on the betrothal of Mary and Joseph from 1504

THE STORY OF MARY

child to be born will be called holy, the Son of God" (Luke 1:34-35).

Gabriel then let Mary know the news about her relative Elizabeth, who had been barren, and Elizabeth's husband, Zacharias. According to the Book of Luke, the angel explained that Elizabeth had conceived a son despite her advanced age and was now in her sixth month of pregnancy: "For nothing will be impossible for God" (Luke 1:37). Mary, who

WHO WAS JOSEPH?

While Joseph could claim royal descent, the Gospels According to Matthew and Mark both refer to him as a carpenter. Yet the Greek word that Mark used is *tektōn* and its meaning is closer to the Aramaic word *naggara*, which means a worker or journeyman. Most of Jesus' parables refer to agriculture, so it is likely that Joseph farmed, with carpentry, which he taught Jesus, as a sideline. He might have even done some work at the nearby city of Sepphoris, a spot that the Jewish historian Flavius Josephus called "the Jewel of Galilee," which was being rebuilt at the time by Herod Antipas.

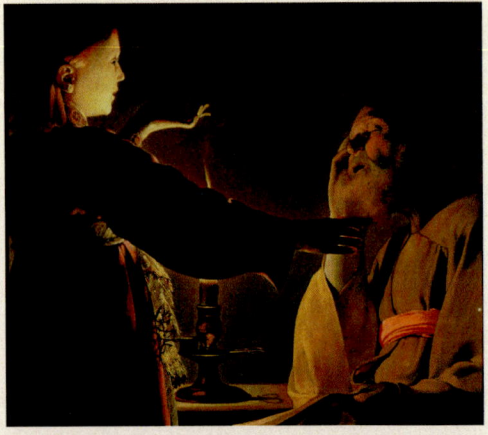

An angel tells Joseph not to leave Mary.

was touched by the divine when she was created free from original sin, acceded to her position, saying to Gabriel, "Behold, I am the handmaid of the Lord. May it be done to me according to your word" (Luke 1:38). She then rushed to Judea to visit Elizabeth. When Elizabeth saw Mary and heard her voice, the unborn child in her womb who would become John the Baptist "leaped for joy" (Luke 1:44).

A PREGNANCY'S IMPLICATIONS

Being pregnant outside marriage could be a dangerous thing. "Once you are betrothed, it is considered adultery," says Carol Meyers, a professor of religion at Duke University. Despite the biblical edict mandating that when "a man commits adultery with his neighbor's wife, both the adulterer and the adulteress shall be put to death" (Leviticus 20:10),

Sepphoris, the royal city near Mary's home in Nazareth, had an amphitheater that seated 4,500 people.

historically, stoning was not always carried out. And there are people mentioned in the Bible who commit such acts and yet are not punished.

Even so, Mary's pregnancy would be looked down upon by the community, and it could also visit

"AS JOSEPH SLUMBERED, AN ANGEL TOLD HIM, "FOR IT IS THROUGH THE HOLY SPIRIT THAT THIS CHILD HAS BEEN CONCEIVED IN HER" (MATTHEW 1:20).

shame on her family. Nazareth was a small place, and neighbors not only knew each other's business but had long communal memories. There were also important social and familial implications for Mary and Joseph. Theirs was a kinship-based society, and a person's identity was established through the father's line, as laid out in the first chapter of the Gospel According to Matthew, which details the male lineage of Jesus' family starting with the patriarch Abraham. Female sexuality was potentially threatening. If a woman had a child outside marriage, her husband would end up caring for a child who was of another man and not of his family

When he was eight days old, Jesus was circumcised as God first commanded Abraham in the Book of Genesis.

line. "They wanted to know that all of those children were of that father," notes McCane, "because he has to support them."

When Joseph learned of his betrothed's pregnancy, he was not happy. But according to the Book of Matthew, Joseph was "a righteous man" (Matthew 1:19). He observed the Bible's commandments and, hoping not to cause Mary any embarrassment, sought to quietly end the erusin. As he thought about how he would do this, he went to sleep. And as he slumbered, Joseph encountered an angel, who told him how, "For it is through the holy Spirit that this child has been conceived in her" (Matthew 1:20). When Joseph awoke, he understood that Mary had been faithful and freely did as the angel bid. They went through with the nissuin and he "took his wife into his home" (Matthew 1:24).

The Gospels According to Matthew and Luke proclaim that as the birth neared, Mary and Joseph traveled to Bethlehem. The Jewish population suffered under a heavy burden of taxes—they owed money to Rome and to King Herod, as well as a tithe of their harvest to the Temple—and the couple, according to Luke, headed there during the census year to pay what had been mandated by Caesar Augustus. The trip would take Mary and Joseph about a week, and the expectant couple probably made their way south along a route where they could stop at springs to rest and find shelter in small towns. When they arrived, Mary went into labor. They needed a place for her to give birth, yet there was no room for them in the inn, so they took refuge in a limestone cave used to corral domesticated animals. The space

A detail from a 14th-century triptych by Duccio di Buoninsegna shows Jesus at rest in the manger.

would have been dark and damp and reeked of manure and hay. After Mary gave birth, she wrapped Jesus in swaddling clothes and set him in a manger, an open trough used to feed the animals. ∎

BETHLEHEM AND NAZARETH

Bethlehem's old quarter

Bethlehem, the storied place of Jesus' birth, is where King David tended his sheep, and his grandson King Rehoboam in the 10th century B.C.E. fortified the town. Nazareth, where Mary raised her son, was a wisp of a village halfway between the Mediterranean Sea and the Sea of Galilee. The city's Church of the Annunciation, the largest in the Middle East, is on the spot where the angel told Mary of her miraculous fate. Archaeologists in 2015 claimed to have found Jesus' home beneath the Sisters of Nazareth Convent, a spot revered by the Byzantines and Crusaders.

THE STORY OF MARY

FLIGHT TO EGYPT

As Jesus entered the world, an angel appeared to the shepherds grazing their flocks in the hills nearby and told them the news: "For today in the city of David a savior has been born for you who is Messiah and Lord" (Luke 2:11). The shepherds rushed over and found the Holy Family with their glorious child named Jesus, Yeshua, which means "God is salvation."

They weren't the only ones seeking out this infant. Wise men from the East had learned of his birth, followed a star, and found the manger. Western tradition holds that there were three Magi, while the Eastern church says there were 12. Whatever the number, the appearance of these well-dressed men must have stunned the Holy Family. Yet the visitors were the ones in awe, for as these gentiles entered and saw Mary cradling her baby, they fell down and worshipped him and presented him with gold, frankincense, and myrrh.

HEROD'S GRAND CITY

On the eighth day Jesus underwent a bris, in fulfillment of the covenant between God and Abraham where God said, "every male among you shall be circumcised" (Genesis 17:10). Following childbirth, a woman was considered "ritually unclean" and "she shall not touch anything sacred nor enter the sanctuary till the days of her purification are fulfilled" (Leviticus 12:4). Mary would have gone to a mikvah, a ritual bath, to cleanse herself. After the allotted number of days, she, Joseph, and Jesus headed to Jerusalem to the Temple—possibly for the *pidyon haben* ceremony for redeeming the first born—to offer a sacrifice to thank God.

Jerusalem was an awe-inspiring place, a city made grand by Herod, who built a palace and rebuilt the Temple. Flavius Josephus wrote that the Temple complex, whose outer court covered 35 acres, stood on the Holy Mount with nine gates "completely overlaid with gold and silver, as were also their door-posts and lintels; but one, that outside the sanctuary, was of Corinthian bronze, and far exceeded in value those plated with silver and set in gold."

"The Temple that Herod built was a showplace," says McCane. Because Herod

A statue of the Good Shepherd, based on one of Jesus' parables

HEROD CREATED A PLACE THAT WAS BOTH A RELIGIOUS DESTINATION FOR THE FAITHFUL AND A TOURIST SPOT FOR THOSE OF OTHER FAITHS AND LANDS.

wanted to appease both his Roman overlords and his Jewish subjects, he created a place that was both a religious destination for the faithful and a tourist spot for those of other faiths and lands. The complex combined the best of Roman architecture with an interior that was distinctively Jewish. "It would have been the most impressive thing they had ever seen."

Like all others coming to the Temple, Mary and Joseph would need an offering, so the family could have stopped in Herod's Royal Stoa, a colonnaded walkway at the Temple's southern end, where merchants sold appropriate sacrificial items. Wealthier supplicants might buy a young lamb. But because Mary and Joseph had little money, they picked up either a pair of turtledoves or two young pigeons.

The family would then have made their way into the Court of the Women, as far as women would be

Giotto di Bondone painted this fresco of the Holy Family, now in the Basilica of St. Francis in Assisi, Italy.

allowed to progress. While the young family visited, the Holy Spirit guided a devout man named Simeon to the Temple. When he saw Jesus, he took the child into his arms and said, "My eyes have seen your salvation" (Luke 2:30), and blessed the family. The widowed prophet Anna also gave thanks and told others of the child.

THE SLAUGHTER OF THE INNOCENTS

Not all rejoiced. Herod had learned of Jesus' birth from the wise men. For Herod, the birth of a child whom the men called "king of the Jews" (Matthew 2:2) was an ill omen. Like Pharaoh in the Book of Exodus, who feared the Israelites' growing strength,

HER EARLY LIFE

Herod ordered the execution of all boys two years old and younger in the region. An angel again appeared to Joseph and told him to flee to Egypt. He and Mary took Jesus and left at night, staying until Herod's death in 4 B.C.E. when an angel told Joseph that it was safe to return to the Holy Land. By then, the Romans had divided the kingdom in thirds, and Herod's son, Herod Archelaus, ruled over most of the Judean kingdom. ■

"The Adoration of the Magi" by the Florentine master Sandro Botticelli, from the 15th century

THE CHURCH OF THE NATIVITY

In the second century, Saint Justin Martyr identified the cave where Mary gave birth to Jesus. During the fourth century, Emperor Constantine and his mother had a basilica built there, which Samaritan rebels destroyed in the sixth century. Emperor Justinian rebuilt it soon after; inside lay the sacred grotto, the spot of the miraculous birth marked by an altar with a 14-point silver star embedded in a marble floor. The site is currently maintained by clergy members of the Roman Catholic, Armenian Apostolic, and Greek Orthodox Churches.

The Church of the Nativity

THE STORY OF MARY

RAISING JESUS

※

The Gospels tell us little about Mary at this time or of Jesus' childhood in Nazareth until he started his ministry. Some denominations believe that Mary had other children. Four brothers are mentioned in the Gospels According to Mark and Matthew—Joseph, Judas, Simon, and James—as well as at least two sisters. Others hold that Joseph was a widower with children.

The other children could also have been Jesus' cousins or relatives, for extended families living together in multifamily homes around a central courtyard was the norm. "It would have been extended family groups. Typically grandpa and grandma, their sons and their wives, and then their children," observes McCane, who codirects a decade-long excavation of a synagogue in nearby Horvat Kur. "Most of the time, it looks like three generations are together."

AN EARLY MIRACLE

These one- or two-room homes were made of stone with the roof held up with wooden beams and a lattice of sticks and boards and packed mud. There, women tended the stoves, washed clothes, and took care of sheep, cattle, and goats. In the Apocrypha Infancy Gospel of Thomas a story tells of Mary doing her chores. She asked Jesus "to draw water and bear it into the house." But as the six-year-old child headed out with the clay jug, others jostled him, and his jug knocked against someone else's container and broke. So when the boy arrived at the well, he "spread out the garment which was upon him" and filled the cloth with water. When Jesus returned, Mary kissed him and wondered why the water did not leak through the fabric, yet "she kept within herself the mysteries which she saw him do."

WOMEN'S WORK

The poor lived on simple diets. They grew barley, and women ground grain with a stone mill. It was hard work. "You had to get down on your hand and knees and rub a stone across grain that

---

THIS PAGE: **A modern Passover seder plate, the sort that might have been used during the Last Supper.** OPPOSITE: **The faithful and tourists visit Jerusalem, the site of the Temple.**

24

The British Pre-Raphaelite painter John Everett Millais's "Christ in the House of His Parents"

was spread on a larger stone in order to make flour. Most women even in well-to-do families had to do this every day," says Meyers. Bread was the main staple of a working-class family's diet, and Mary would have started the morning by kneading and then baking flat round breads in a oven. Roughly 60 to 70 percent of a person's daily caloric intake would be some form of grain, so women produced a huge amount of food every day.

For breakfast, the family ate the bread, possibly with some goat or sheep cheese, as well as olives. At midday, they had bread as well as figs, olives, and other grains. For dinner, Mary could prepare a stew

> **BREAD** WAS THE **MAIN STAPLE** OF A WORKING-CLASS FAMILY'S DIET, AND MARY WOULD HAVE STARTED THE MORNING BY **KNEADING** AND **BAKING** FLAT ROUND BREADS.

made with lentils, chickpeas, and herbs, the liquid sopped up with more bread. Fish from the Sea of Galilee—which abounded with *musht,* or St. Peter's fish, carp, and sardines—was also popular. Food would be served with wine. "People didn't have meat

HER EARLY LIFE

very often except for a holiday and maybe on the Sabbath," says Meyers, at which time they could have a chance to enjoy some lamb or goat.

Courtyards, especially those of civic leaders, doubled as synagogues, with benches set on the stone or beaten earth floor and congregants probably using an Aramaic translation of the Bible. Jesus knew how to read, and it is possible that Mary sent him to learn in such a space. Called *Bet ha-Sefer,* these places offered primary education in Scriptures.

Twelve-year-old Jesus discussing the Bible with scholars at the Temple following his Passover pilgrimage

JESUS' HOME

Archaeologists recently claimed to have found Jesus' childhood home. The location sits beneath the Sister of Nazareth Convent, a place long considered the spot where Jesus grew up, one revered by the Byzantines and Crusaders. The area was excavated by the Nazareth Archaeological Project, whose scholars cited a reference by a Scottish abbot who visited there in the seventh century and wrote that it is "where once there was the house in which the Lord was nourished in his infancy." When the project dug down, they discovered a first-century courtyard house.

A site believed to be Jesus' home

PASSOVER IN JERUSALEM

Because Mary and Joseph were devout, each year they made the long trip to Jerusalem to celebrate Passover. When Jesus was 12, the family went there, possibly with relatives and friends. As they headed home, they didn't notice their son's absence. When they discovered him gone, they searched and found him still in the Temple. There, Jesus sat with the scholars on Solomon's Porch in a discussion about the Torah. When Mary told him how she was worried and that "your father and I have been looking for you with great anxiety," Jesus responded, "Why were you looking for me? Did you not know that I must be in my Father's house?" (Luke 2:48-49).

They didn't quite understand what he said, but when they made it back to Nazareth, Mary could not fail to notice how her son continued to grow not only in height but also in wisdom. ∎

CHAPTER 2

Mary's Times
THE WORLD OF THE BIBLE

The Holy Family traced its ancestry to the kingdom of David. The book of Samuel relates the story of the shepherd from the tribe of Judah who armed himself with five stones and with his slingshot smote the Philistine Goliath. David soon became a towering leader who united the tribes of Israel.

As king, David penned the Psalms and set off the Jewish golden age by besting the Philistines and capturing Jerusalem from the Jebusites, a Canaanite tribe. It was here in the Judean Mountains that David established his legendary capital. To Jerusalem, he brought the Ark of the Covenant containing the sacred stone tablets God bestowed on Moses and the Israelites at Mount Sinai. David's son Solomon made it a grand capital by setting his famed Temple on Jerusalem's Mount Moriah. He erected great public works, established Israelite colonies in Syria, and created a trading empire.

But when Solomon's son Rehoboam assumed the throne, he favored their tribe of Judah. The northern ten tribes split off to create the Northern Kingdom of Israel; the Southern Kingdom became home to the tribes of Judah and Benjamin. The Assyrian Empire conquered the north in the mid-eighth century B.C.E. and, according to the historian Josephus, took those tribes "beyond the Euphrates," where they became lost to history. One hundred fifty years later, the Babylonian leader Nebuchadrezzar II invaded the south, destroyed Solomon's Temple, and exiled the tribes of Judah and Benjamin. The Persian ruler Cyrus the Great defeated that empire around 538 and allowed the Jews to return home. Once there, they rebuilt the Temple.

ABOVE: **A first-century statue of toga-clad men, who might have been Roman senators.**
OPPOSITE: **Herod the Great's impenetrable palace complex at Masada in the Judean Desert.**

THE LIVES THEY LED

Except for Jerusalem, Sepphoris, and a few other cities, the regions of Judea in the south, Galilee in the north, and Samaria in between had agricultural economies. Homes had to be self-sustaining, and women began work before dawn and didn't finish until after sunset. Women also helped their husbands with the backbreaking work of plowing, planting, tending, and harvesting crops.

WOMEN AND THE HOME

At home, most women oversaw small kitchen gardens; tended to whatever livestock they had, from goats to chickens; maintained the storage of food and other goods; and produced textiles and pottery. As a household's matriarch, Mary would have had a life centered on caring for her family, following the strict biblical dietary laws for the preparation and serving of food, and ensuring that all was in order during the week for the arrival of the Sabbath. "All those things are things that women were almost exclusively in charge of," observes Professor Carol Meyers.

Religion constituted a basic component of everyday life, and Mary would have watched over the religious upbringing of her son. Just as Mary had learned the prayers and rituals of daily observance from her mother, Anne, and the others around her, she would have imparted the same lessons to Jesus and those in her household. And though the lives of women might be circumscribed, they had rights at home and within the community, though not on the same scale as men. For example, they could own property, and there are records of women initiating divorces.

> "DURING THEIR VISIT, **MARY AND JOSEPH** PURCHASED **TWO SMALL BIRDS** THAT THEY GAVE TO THE PRIEST AT THE TEMPLE TO **PERFORM THE SACRIFICE.**

THE ANCIENT ECONOMY

Economies were simple and revolved around agricultural cycles and the harvest. People like Mary and Joseph were self-sufficient; they raised such crops as barley, wheat, and oats; survived in a barter society; and would have had limited contact with currency. But it is likely that they came across coinage in Nazareth, when visiting Sepphoris, or when they headed to the Temple in Jerusalem following Jesus' birth.

A reconstruction of the sort of loom that Mary could have used at her home in Nazareth

THE STORY OF MARY

During that visit, Mary and Joseph purchased the two small birds that they gave to the priest at the Temple to perform the sacrifice in order to express thanks to God. One of the coins they might have handled there could have been a prutah, a low-value

MARY MAGDALENE, JOANNA, AND SUSANNA

Luke relates that as Jesus preached, women whom he'd cured accompanied him. He names three, Mary Magdalene, Joanna, and Susanna, whom Jesus freed from evil spirits and infirmities and who became his benefactors. Mary, who most likely came from Magdala on the Sea of Galilee, was the most famous. He exorcised her of "seven demons" (Luke 8:2). Mary, who has often been wrongly portrayed as his wife or as a prostitute, not only witnessed his Crucifixion but was the first to see him following the Resurrection.

Jesus' disciple, Mary Magdalene

coin. King Herod was an Edomite who practiced Judaism. He rebuilt the Temple, and was cognizant of the beliefs of both the ruling religious classes in Jerusalem and the sensitivity of average citizens like Mary. So he had the prutah and other coins struck with such images as an eagle instead of his own profile in the hope of not offending Jews with the creation of graven images.

32

The fertile Galilean land where Mary and Joseph lived and through which Jesus led his historic ministry

THREE FESTIVALS

The family would regularly return to Jerusalem because God in Deuteronomy commanded the Jews to visit there three times a year for what are called the Shalosh Regalim, or the Three Pilgrimages. There is the arrival for Shavuot, an agricultural celebration in late spring. In the fall they would have come to mark Sukkot, a harvest holiday that celebrates the Jews' 40 years of wandering in the desert on the way to the Promised Land. And in the spring they would go to Jerusalem for Passover, a week-long holiday recalling the Jews' liberation from Egyptian slavery more than a thousand years earlier.

> **WOMEN** WERE INVOLVED WITH **THEIR SYNAGOGUES.** SOME UPPER-CLASS WOMEN HAD **LEADERSHIP ROLES** IN THEIR **COMMUNITIES' RELIGIOUS LIFE.**

Festivals during each of the three holidays attracted tens of thousands from villages and towns throughout the lands. The supplicants traveled there by foot, horse, and donkey and rested in inns. To accommodate so many people, Herod built a vast courtyard around the Temple.

Jerusalem was far away and a special visit for most women like Mary. "If you lived in Nazareth you never, if ever—male or female—can spend much time at the Temple," says Meyers. Since the Temple was not a significant part of the day-to-day religiosity of the kingdom's people, most took part in spiritual life on a basic local level. By the Roman era, small synagogues, *beit knesets,* had spread throughout the land, offering people some kind of focus or access to communal Jewish life. Mary's hometown had one: The Book of Luke mentions that after Jesus spent 40 days in the desert and started his ministry, he returned to Nazareth, attended Sabbath services, and stood up and read from the Book of Isaiah.

A reconstruction of a third-century c.e. home in Katzrin in the Golan Heights northeast of Galilee

WOMEN AND RELIGIOUS LIFE

Men ran religious services, but women not only attended but also sat with the men. Judaism in the first-century Roman period was not restrictive for women as is usually believed; the separation of the sexes did not occur until much later. Women were also involved with their synagogues. Some upper-class women had leadership and sponsorship roles in their communities' religious life.

While it's unlikely that a working-class woman like Mary of Nazareth would have been a leader, she would have seen other women who were. And as is evidenced in the Gospels, Jewish women served as some of her son's most devoted and helpful followers, offering much-needed support during his wide-ranging travels.

Religion was thus tightly integrated into daily life. Jews of that period not only focused on observing dietary laws but also followed specific rules found in the Bible for maintaining cleanliness. Mikvahs were used not only to purify people, as Mary would have done following Jesus' birth, but possibly to cleanse vessels and clothing.

MIKVAHS AND DAILY LIFE

Archaeologists working throughout Israel have found the remains of some 700 mikvahs, an indication of its centrality to daily life. Most Judean villages had utilitarian facilities with steps leading down to the bath, and some communities had numerous such facilities. The largest number of baths have been found in Jerusalem. Some 200 mikvahs have been uncovered there, including one wealthy family's in-home bath with a barrel-vaulted ceiling, ornate window, and cistern. ∎

A fifth-century B.C.E. *ketubah*. Such Jewish marriage licenses list a man's responsibilities. This one was written in Aramaic.

MARY'S SPRING

Located just west of Jerusalem in Ein Kerem—Arabic for "spring of the vineyard"—between the Church of Saint John and the Church of the Visitation flows a spring. It is believed Mary stopped there for a cool drink before visiting her pregnant relative Elizabeth. While there, she supposedly said the Magnificat found in Luke:

> My soul proclaims the greatness of the Lord;
> my spirit rejoices in God my savior.
> For he has looked upon his handmaid's lowliness; behold, from now on will all ages call me blessed (Luke 1:46-48).

Mary's Spring, where the Virgin stopped for water

THE STORY OF MARY

THE ROMAN OCCUPATION

In the shifting fortunes of the Mediterranean that would give rise to the world of Mary, Joseph, and Jesus, Alexander the Great defeated the Persians in 332 B.C.E. and took over Judea. When he died, his generals carved up his empire. Judea first fell under the control of the Ptolemys and then the Seleucids, which followed Alexander's example by promoting Greek culture.

When the Seleucid King Antiochus IV assumed the throne, he sought to rid the land of opposing religions and spread across his realm a common culture. He denigrated Jewish practices, called for the construction of shrines, and forbade the observance of the Sabbath. According to the historian Josephus, those who disagreed were "crucified while they lived and breathed." Then in the 160s B.C.E., his troops plundered and desecrated the Temple. The priest Mattathias Maccabee from the village of Modi'in resented this abomination. Leading his five sons, he rallied a guerrilla resistance against their occupiers.

HANUKKAH

Mattathias's son Judas soon took over the fight, joining his troops prior to battle in prayer. Around 164 B.C.E., they recaptured Jerusalem. There they reconsecrated the Temple and adorned the front with crowns of gold. Legend has it that when they arrived, they had only enough oil to light the menorah for one night. Yet miraculously, the oil lasted for eight nights, the event recalled during the holiday of Hanukkah, which means "dedication."

JUDEA'S INDEPENDENCE

The struggle over Judea continued even after the Maccabees reclaimed the capital. It wasn't until Mattathias's son Simon ruled that he founded the Hasmonean dynasty and the kingdom became independent. His son John became known as Hyrcanus I. He served as high priest and expanded the kingdom, adding Samaria and Idomaea, and converting the local Edomites, an Arab tribe to which the future King Herod's family belonged.

But while the Hasmonean family had initially set out to battle Greek influence, they had become Hellenized and scoffed at the

Alexander the Great's army defeated the Persians and conquered Judea in 332 B.C.E.

36

In the Vatican is Raphael's fresco of Heliodorus being expelled from the Temple during the Maccabean Revolt.

> **THE STRUGGLE OVER JUDEA** CONTINUED EVEN AFTER THE MACCABEES RECLAIMED THE CAPITAL. IT WASN'T UNTIL **SIMON RULED** THAT IT BECAME INDEPENDENT.

practices of many of their own subjects. Alexander Jannaeus, who ruled from 103 B.C.E. to 76 B.C.E., was an especially cruel leader. He performed a Temple ceremony incorrectly in order to show disrespect to the beliefs of some. When the crowd voiced their displeasure by pelting him with *etrogim,* citrus fruit used during the holiday of Sukkot, he had his troops slaughter 6,000 of them.

JUDEA AND ROME

Alexander Jannaeus's wife, Salome Alexandra, succeeded him. When she died, their sons, Aristobulus II and John Hyrcanus II, fought over the kingdom and the Temple. The fight came at the same time that the Roman senate sought to expand the republic's power into the Near East. As Aristobulus was besieged in the Temple, he appealed to Gnaeus Pompeius Magnus, the general known as Pompey, who had just captured Damascus. As an enticement for support, he sent Pompey 17,600 pounds of silver.

But Pompey soon sided with Hyrcanus. Using battering rams and stone-hurling catapults, the general's troops smashed into the Temple terrace. As they assaulted the complex, priests committed suicide, and troops massacred some 12,000 people.

The general and his men then entered the Temple's most sacred space, the Holy of Holies. The next day, Pompey had the high priest Hyrcanus stripped of his royal status.

Judea became a client kingdom of Rome. At that time, the Holy Land was just a small part of that empire's vast collection of states, which stretched from Northern Africa up to the British Isles and across to Syria. These were the last years of the nearly 500-year-old Roman Republic. And just as disorder and anarchy reigned during the Hasmonean's rule, there was much turmoil and machinations with those who hoped to control Rome.

AN EMPIRE IS BORN

The Edomite chieftain Antipater could see the benefits of siding with the Romans, and supported Pompey during his invasion. In 60 B.C.E., Pompey, Julius Caesar, and Marcus Licinius Crassus established the First Triumvirate. But a civil war between Caesar and his former ally and son-in-law Pompey broke out in 49 B.C.E. Pompey was killed, and Antipater then pledged his allegiance to Caesar. In 47 B.C.E., he became procurator of Judea. He in turn made his son Herod governor of Galilee and his other son Phasael governor of Judea and Perea.

Caesar took over as dictator in 46 B.C.E. and was assassinated two years later. This led to another triumvirate formed with Caesar's nephew, Octavian, the general Mark Antony, and the statesman Marcus Aemilius Lepidus. But Octavian and Antony fought. Soon after beating Antony in a naval battle at Actium off the coast of Greece in 31 B.C.E., Octavian became the sole master of the Roman world, took on the name Augustus, and extinguished the Republic forever. ∎

The lighting of the candles on Hanukkah celebrates a joyous holiday that recalls the Maccabees' victory over the Seleucids.

ROMAN PALESTINE

- Roman province of Palestina
- Roman province of Syria
- Roman province of Arabia
- ○ Location uncertain
- [Jerusalem] Former city name

MARE INTERNUM (MEDITERRANEAN SEA)

Sidon
Damascus
Mt. Hermon 2,814 m / 9,232 ft
Tyre
Caesarea Philippi
Kanah
Cadasa
Ecdippa
Asor
Raphana
Merom
GAULANITIS
Ptolemais
Bay of Acco (Bay of Haifa)
Capernaum
Bethsaida
Jotapata
Laus Tiberias (Sea of Galilee)
Sycaminium
Arbela
Mt. Carmel 546 m / 1,791 ft
Tiberias
Hippos
Gabae
Sepphoris
Nazareth
Philoteria
Dora
Legio
Mt. Tabor 588 m / 1,929 ft
Gadara
Abila
Caesarea
Scythopolis
Pella
Narbata
Ginae
°Dion
Mt. Ebal 940 m / 3,084 ft
Gerasa
Apollonia
Sebaste
Neapolis
Amathus
Mt. Gerizim 881 m / 2,890 ft
Joppa
Antipatris
Lebonah
Phasaelis
Gadara
Lydda
Bethel
Archelais
Philadelphia
Jamnia
Gazara
Emmaus
Jericho
Esbus
Azotus
Aelia Capitolina [Jerusalem]
Bethany
Mt. Nebo 802 m / 2,631 ft
Medeba
Bethlehem
Ascalon
Marisa
Beth-zur
Lachish
Hebron
Anthedon
Gaza
Eshtemoa
'En-gedi
Lacus Asphaltitis (Dead Sea)
Raphia
Beersheba
Kir-Moab

NEGEV

EGYPT

0 — 20 — 40 kilometers
0 — 20 — 40 miles

Present-day drainage, coastlines, and country boundaries are represented.

THE STORY OF MARY

THE ROMAN EMPIRE

- Area ruled by the time of Julius Caesar's death, 44 B.C.E.
- Gains by the time of Caesar Augustus' death, 14 C.E.
- Gains by Emperor Trajan, 117 C.E.
- Region temporarily held by Rome, with dates
- Fortified frontier
- Roman road
- ✷ Empire capital
- ⊙ Provincial capital
- ◯ Legion headquarters
- ⚓ Major naval base

40

MARY'S TIMES

THE STORY OF MARY

HEROD THE GREAT

Like his father Antipater, Herod saw where power resided. He owed his position to Rome. So when the Parthians, a Persian empire, swept in and conquered Judea in 40 B.C.E., Herod headed to Italy in search of support. There he stated his case in front of the Senate. The senators were so taken by Herod that they named him king of Judea and equipped him with an army.

Landing in Acre, Herod conquered the kingdom in 37 B.C.E., not long before the birth of Mary. When Augustus took control of Rome, Herod, who had been friends with Mark Antony, headed to Rhodes to pledge his fealty. The king of Judea appeared without his crown to show humility, and Augustus rewarded Herod. "The Romans deliberately did not chose a Hasmonean or a Maccabee to be king because that would cater to Jewish nationalist aspiration," says Shaye J. D. Cohen, a professor of Hebrew literature and philosophy at Harvard. "They picked somebody who is in between, sort of one foot in, one foot out."

As an Edomite, a member of a Semitic group that converted to Judaism in the second century B.C.E., Herod still needed to appease the local populace, which viewed him with suspicion. To strengthen his internal ties, Herod divorced his wife, Doris, and married into the Hasmonean royal family by taking Princess Mariamne as his wife.

A Machiavellian leader who, according to the Book of Matthew, called for the Massacre of the Innocents following Jesus' birth, Herod proved highly paranoid. He had informers and executed all he believed plotted against him. He had his brother-in-law, the high priest Aristobulus, drowned, and killed Mariamne, whom he delusionally thought was unfaithful, along with her two sons, her mother, Alexandra, and grandfather, and Antipater, his son by Doris.

A GRAND KINGDOM

Despite his murderous ways, Herod ensured the independence of the Jews of his land and strengthened the economy. During the great famine of 25 B.C.E., he fed his people by shipping in wheat from Egypt. He oversaw a massive building program with grand cities and imposing fortresses. Yet while the economy boomed, many Jews were forced into labor to raise his grand structures, like the acropolis at Samaria and his desert palace fortress at Masada.

An oil lamp from the time of Herod. The small light used a wick to burn olive oil.

42

Herod's winter palace near Jericho had baths decorated with frescoes that looked like marble.

The king's most ambitious project was the port of Caesarea Maritima so that his land could claim a major harbor to attract trade. Caesarea, south of present-day Jaffa and Haifa, also served as the administrative center of the province and was where Pontius Pilate, the governor and prefect who ordered Jesus' execution, lived. It had an amphitheater, which held 20,000, and a Roman temple dedicated to Augustus and the goddess Roma.

But while Caesarea was imposing, the Temple in Jerusalem stands as Herod's crowning glory. Work began on enlarging the complex in 20 B.C.E. Herod rebuilt the site as a way to show his strength but also to increase the presence and prestige of Judaism within that empire. His Greco-Roman temple sat on a huge platform, and Josephus wrote that it was made of finely hewn white stones 20 cubits long and six cubits high.

When Herod died in 4 B.C.E. after a long illness—a death that allowed Mary, Joseph, and Jesus to return to Galilee—he was buried with great ceremony in the mausoleum he constructed in his fortress of Herodium near Jerusalem. During the procession, 500 servants carried spices, and according to Josephus, the king was buried "covered with purple; and a diadem was put upon his head, and a crown of gold above it, and a scepter in his right hand." ∎

JEWISH RELIGIOUS SECTS

There was no uniformity in Judaism at this time, and the period when Jesus of Nazareth came of age was rife with religious tensions. Some groups adhered to unbending beliefs in the written law, others took a larger view, and some embraced apocalyptic ideas. Holy men and healers walked the land, as did Jesus, whose teachings his followers would soon spread.

Two main religious groups are discussed in the New Testament, the Sadducees and the Pharisees. The Sadducees could trace their ancestry back to David's high priest, Zadok. Making up a conservative and haughty sliver of society, they aligned themselves with the Romans and were composed of not only the priestly class but also aristocrats and merchants. They ran the Temple, oversaw ritual sacrifices, controlled the Sanhedrin—the supreme religious council—and were responsible for collecting tithes for the Temple.

THE SADDUCEES

As fundamentalist adherents to the Torah, the five books of Moses, the Sadducees followed a literal interpretation of the Bible. They therefore took a severe stance on crime and punishment, following the edict in Exodus of an eye for an eye and a tooth for a tooth. They did not embrace the growing belief of an afterlife, since it is not mentioned in the Torah. This is evident when the Book of Matthew noted an exchange between the Sadducees and Jesus. And it was their running of the Temple that Jesus opposed when he cast out the money changers.

> **THE PHARISEES WERE MADE UP OF PIOUS SCHOLARS AND LAYMEN. THEIR BELIEFS APPEALED TO THE MAJORITY OF JEWS.**

After the Romans destroyed the Temple in 70 C.E., the Sadducees vanished.

THE PHARISEES

The Pharisees were made up of pious scholars and laymen. Their beliefs appealed to the majority of Jews. The Book of Luke mentioned that Jesus dined with one, and the apostle Paul started as a Pharisee, having studied with Gamaliel of Jerusalem, a renowned scholar. The Pharisees sought to adapt old laws to current issues. As a result, they believed

---

A scene from Harold Copping's 1907 "The Question of the Sadducees"

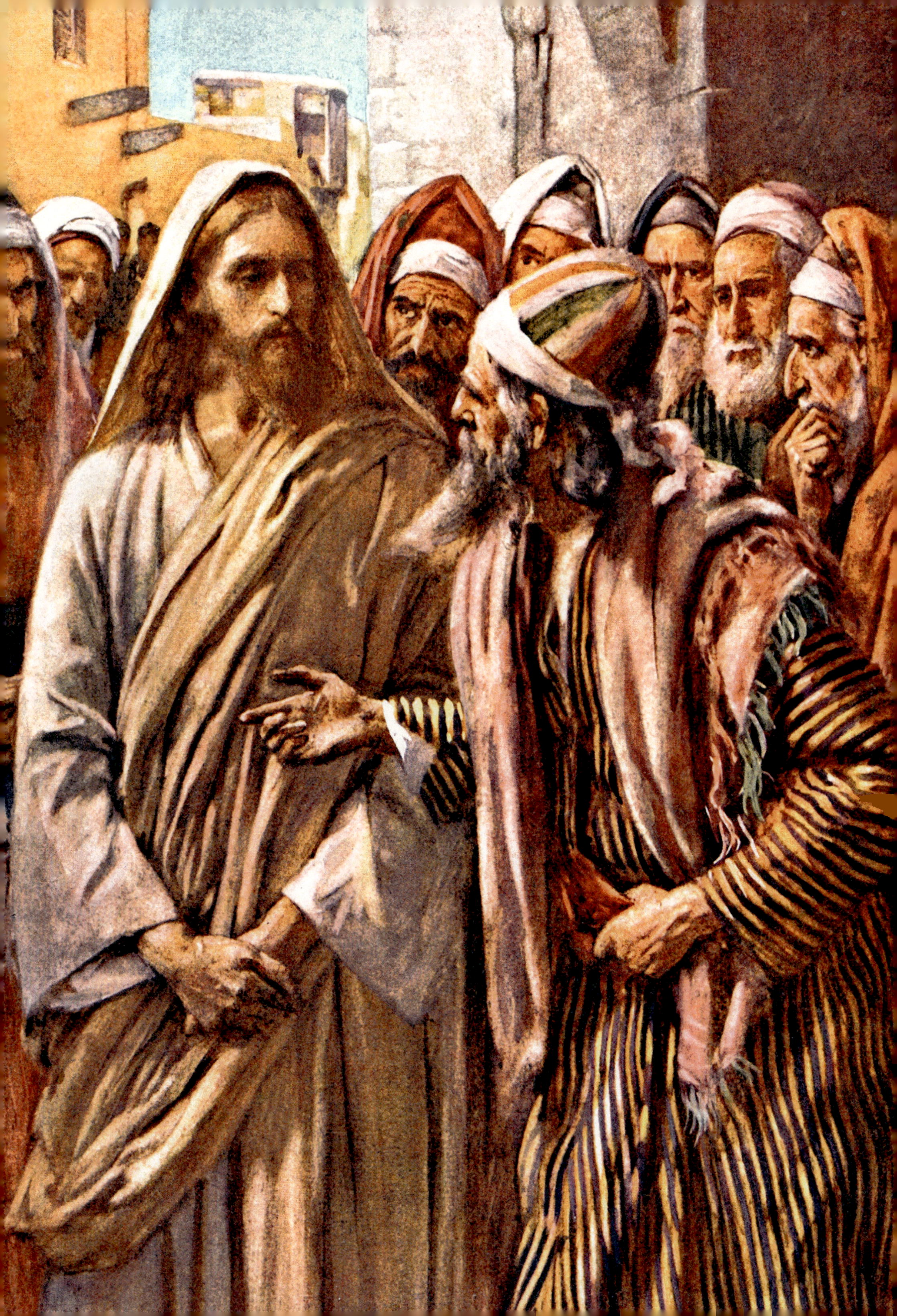

THE STORY OF MARY

> IT IS POSSIBLE THAT **THE ESSENES CREATED THE DEAD SEA SCROLLS, A TREASURE TROVE** OF **BIBLICAL WRITINGS** LEFT IN THE JUDEAN DESERT.

JERUSALEM AND THE TEMPLE

King Solomon set the Jerusalem Temple on the spot where Abraham nearly sacrificed his son Isaac. The Babylonians destroyed the building, and the Israelites built a new one; Herod expanded the complex. It was there during his time in Jerusalem that Jesus expelled the money changers. After General Titus conquered Jerusalem in 70, he was honored with a triumphal arch in Rome. It still stands in the eternal city and contains a relief showing soldiers carrying off the Temple's menorah.

The Temple's Royal Stoa

---

in following both God's law, which Moses received at Mount Sinai, and the oral law that came from traditions and the knowledge imparted by the prophets.

Instead of the sacrifices that the Sadducees emphasized, the Pharisees believed that the way to please God was through ritual purity. And since God existed everywhere, he could be worshipped through prayer and study outside the Temple. They therefore promoted the synagogues, an idea that helped make them an integral part of Jewish society. After General Titus destroyed Jerusalem in 70 C.E., it was the synagogues and the schools inside them that continued to nurture the Jewish people.

THE ESSENES

The Essenes were a small, monastic group. Josephus wrote that they abandoned the cities and lived in the country in order to be closer to God. Similar to the Pharisees in their belief in ritual purity, they built cisterns fed by local springs to make possible daily ritual immersions. They adhered to the laws of Moses and believed in the idea of immortality. Out away from the rest of Judean society, the Essenes lived ascetic, communal lives, wore long robes, worked the land, devoted themselves to the study of scriptures, and prayed throughout the Sabbath.

THE DEAD SEA SCROLLS

It is possible that the Essenes created the Dead Sea Scrolls, a treasure trove of biblical writings. These scriptures were stored in clay jars and seem to have been left in the Qumran caves in the Judean Desert as the Roman legions approached in 68 C.E. The group and their writings were forgotten until a Bedouin shepherd searching for a lost member of his flock stumbled on some scrolls in 1947. Over the subsequent decades, Bedouins and archaeologists have discovered more than 800 manuscripts covering the Old Testament and other works, all offering an unparalleled view into that lost and forgotten world. ∎

THIS PAGE: **A coin depicting the Temple.** OPPOSITE: **A detail of a scene where Herod receives the head of John the Baptist.**

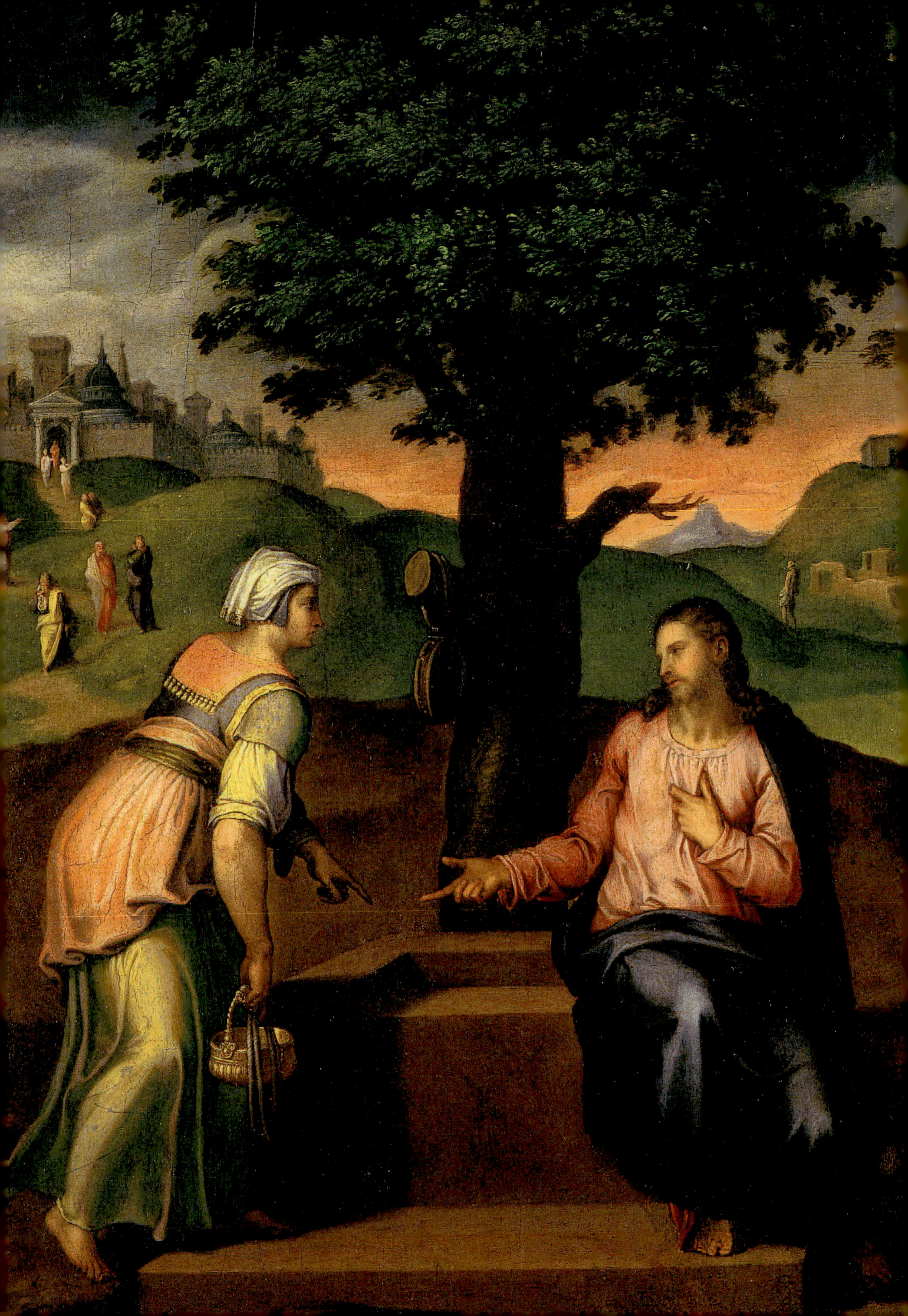

CHAPTER 3

Jesus Comes of Age
THE MOTHER OF THE MESSIAH

There is a large time gap in the Gospels, so we do not know what happened to Mary, Joseph, and Jesus between their visit to Jerusalem over Passover and when Jesus was grown. The story picks up again with Elizabeth and Zacharias's miracle son, who would become known as John the Baptist.

John led a spartan life and may have spent time with the Essenes. Like the members of that ascetic group living in the Judean desert, John dressed modestly and survived simply on honey and locusts, a crunchy food that is considered kosher.

As with the Essenes, John believed in the approaching apocalypse. He warned all who had neglected Jewish law that God's judgment would soon rain down. They needed to repent and be cleansed of their sins through baptism. Many heeded John's call, and his followers undertook penitent fasting and recited special prayers.

John's evangelical journey took him to Bethany on the eastern shore of the Jordan River. One day Jesus came there seeking baptism. John dipped him into the river, and as Jesus rose from the water, the heavens opened. God's spirit descended and a voice said, "This is my beloved Son" (Matthew 3:17).

That spirit sent Jesus into the wilderness, where he prepared for his new life. There he spent 40 days, like the Jews' 40 years in the desert, Moses' 40 days at Mount Sinai, and the 40 days that the Israelites spied on Canaan before entering their new home. He fasted, was tempted by Satan, and was ministered to by angels. And when he emerged, he was ready to begin his ministry.

ABOVE: **An earthenware plate with a depression used for a popular fish sauce.**
OPPOSITE: **In a scene from the Book of John, Jesus meets a Samaritan woman at a well and asks her for some water.**

MARY DURING JESUS' MINISTRY

Though Mary is central to the story of Jesus' birth and childhood and appears when Roman soldiers crucify him, there is little written about her during the one- to three-year period her son traveled, preached, and cured people. And while there is some limited discussion of Mary at this time, Joseph disappeared from the narrative following the family's Jerusalem visit.

Joseph was likely older than Mary when they married. The Protoevangelium of James quotes him as saying he should not be considered as a husband for the young girl because "I am an old man." So by the time Jesus was around 30 and set off to see John the Baptist, Mary was probably a widow.

THE WIDOW MARY

When women married, they became part of their husband's family. So as a widow, Mary would have counted on those in that extended household for help. It is also likely that there were other children in the household; the Gospels refer to Jesus' four brothers as well as his sisters. Whether they were siblings, stepsiblings, or cousins is impossible to determine, but they probably provided support.

Life at the time was hard, and widowhood could have been an especially harsh burden. This was despite the Bible's injunctions protecting widows, such as the passage in Deuteronomy calling for giving a tithing to them, as well as commandments against mistreating widows, with God warning those who disobeyed him that "my wrath will flare up" (Exodus 22:23).

In the Bible, some widows without support are the recipients of miracles. In the second book of Kings, for example, the prophet Elisha helped a poor widow who possessed only one pot of oil and feared that her creditor would enslave her sons. Elisha then caused the oil to increase, giving her enough to sell and repay her debts. And Luke reported Jesus' compassion for a woman who had just lost her son: When he touched the funeral bier, the son rose and spoke.

THE WEDDING AT CANA

We can only wonder what Mary's life might have been like without Joseph as Jesus started his preaching. We do know from the Gospel According to John, though, that she encouraged her son to perform his first miracle soon after

A leather-and-fiber basket, which was probably used to hold personal items

> **LIFE AT THE TIME WAS HARD,** AND WIDOWHOOD COULD HAVE BEEN A HARSH BURDEN, **DESPITE THE BIBLE'S INJUNCTIONS** PROTECTING WIDOWS.

he emerged from the desert. Mary was in Cana for a wedding, and Jesus attended the festivities with his disciples. It appears to have been a large affair, and at one point, the wine ran out.

When Mary asked Jesus for help, he responded harshly, saying, "Woman, how does your concern affect me? My hour has not yet come" (John 2:4). He seemed to indicate that he wasn't ready to reveal who he was and what he was capable of. Yet despite Jesus' retort, Mary turned to the nearby servants and told them to do whatever he requested. Jesus then instructed the servants to fill six large stone jars with

The mosaic "Prayer in the Garden" at Ravenna's Basilica of Sant'Apollinare Nuovo

water. Once they did, he said they should serve it to the man running the feast. They did as he ordered, and out came wine, which tasted quite good.

THE SITE OF THE CELEBRATION

Two sites have been identified as that wedding's possible location. Visitors often visit Kefer, near Nazareth, where stands the Franciscan Wedding Church, and shops sell varieties of "Cana Wedding Wine."

THE STORY OF MARY

Veronese's 16th-century depiction of the Wedding at Cana includes images of France's King Francis I.

The community, though, lacks Roman-era ruins, and this is one reason why others consider the true location of Cana to be Khirbet Qana, meaning "the ruins of Cana." The spot is located on an isolated hilltop overlooking the Beth Netofa Valley some eight miles north of Nazareth and 10 miles west of the Sea of Galilee. Archaeologists believe that at the time of Jesus, Khirbet Qana covered some 10 acres and had about 1,200 people. Excavations there have uncovered Roman-era homes, tombs, several mikvahs, and possibly a synagogue.

FAMILY REDEFINED

Mary is referenced a number of times when Jesus is being spoken about, and someone comments that he is her son. By then, Jesus is traveling, with crowds seeking cures flocking to him from all over Galilee, Judea, Idumea, Jordan, Tyre, and Sidon. They pressed him to free them of palsy, withered hands, fevers, leprosy, and unclean spirits. He worked constantly, curing on the Sabbath, breaking bread with sinners, and meeting tax collectors.

While he spread his ministry, he also attracted the unwanted attention of state and religious leaders. While Jesus defended his actions, Mary, members of his family, and friends worried that his actions could be viewed as challenging Roman and Jewish authorities. It was at this point, as he was curing the crippled, the blind, and others, that Mary's only other appearance during his ministry occurs. It is quite brief but shows her concern for her son. Mary and the rest of his family came to see Jesus and someone told him, "Your mother and your brothers are standing outside, asking to speak with you." Jesus answered matter-of-factly, "Who is my mother? Who are my brothers?" He then pointed toward his disciples and distanced himself from his birth family by saying, "Here are my mother and my brothers. For whoever does the will of my heavenly Father is my brother, and sister, and mother" (Matthew 12:47-50). ■

JESUS COMES OF AGE

THE TRAVELS OF JESUS

Legend:
- Ruled by Herod Antipas
- Ruled by Herod Philip
- Roman province of Judea
- Roman province of Syria
- Imperial estate
- Nabatean Kingdom
- .... District or region boundary
- → Route of Joseph, Mary, and Jesus during Herod's time
- ← Return route from Egypt
- ← Probable routes for regular trips to Jerusalem
- ← Jesus' final journey to Jerusalem
- • / ○ City of the Decapolis / location uncertain
- [Paneas] Former name of city

On a trip to the area around Tyre and Sidon, Jesus healed the daughter of a gentile woman. (Matthew 15:21-28)

Simon Peter gave his great confession, "You are the Messiah, the Son of the living God." Jesus had asked who the people thought he was. (Matthew 16:13-20)

THE STORY OF MARY

JESUS' DISCIPLES

Many itinerant holy men and revolutionaries made their way around the villages and towns of Judea and Galilee. There were miracle workers like Hanina ben Dosa. A man named Theudas claimed he could part the waters of the River Jordan. A leader called the Egyptian Prophet said he could cause the walls of Jerusalem to tumble. And Judas the Galilean fought against Roman taxes.

But while preachers, healers, and others agitated and roamed the land, there was clearly something different about Jesus that attracted so many. Mary was the first to sense the preternatural wonder of her son when he was still young, marveling at his knowledge when he met with the scholars in the Temple. She served as his first teacher and instilled in him core values. At Cana, she watched him perform his first miracle. She then stayed with him until the end. Because of this, she can be considered his first disciple.

Although Mary seems to be absent during much of her son's travels, he wasn't alone. For after Jesus left his home and spent 40 days in the desert, he headed to Capernaum, a community on the northern shore of the Sea of Galilee that lay along a major trade route. There Jesus started to preach and amass his group of 12 disciples, a number believed to be inspired by the original tribes of Israel. These men were called the apostles; the name comes from the Greek word *apostolos,* which appropriately means a "person sent."

A few of them worked as fishermen. As Jesus walked along the water, he met Peter, also called Simon, and his brother Andrew, a follower of John the Baptist (who had been killed by Herod Antipas). He called to them, and they set down their nets and followed him. Two other brothers, James, also known as James the Greater, and John, who would become known as John the Evangelist and John the Divine, also went along. Philip, another follower of John the Baptist, hailed from Bethsaida in present-day Jordan. His friend Bartholomew, whom Jesus said lacked guile, came from Cana.

There was Thomas, who was also called Judas Thomas and would be dubbed Doubting Thomas because he at first refused to believe in Jesus' Resurrection. Matthew worked as a publican, a local tax collector for Herod Antipas. When Jesus asked Matthew to follow him, he immediately quit his job.

A first-century C.E. bronze brooch with the insignia of Rome's 10th Legion

James the Lesser or the Younger lived in Galilee. His brother, who was called both Thaddaeus and Jude, preached throughout Judea, Samaria, and other areas after Jesus' death.

AN ADVANCE TEAM

There was Simon, who was also known as Simon the Zealot. And there was Judas Iscariot. He may have come from Kerioth in Judea and might have belonged to a radical Jewish group called the Sicarii that sought to expel the Romans. It was Judas Iscariot who would betray the apostles' leader to the Romans.

Jesus used the apostles as a sort of advance scouting party, sending them out in pairs to communities to see if residents would welcome them, telling them to seek the charity of others and admonishing them to travel simply with just a coat, staff, and sandals. In return, the men received the honor of watching and learning from Jesus, and he granted them the power to cast out unclean spirits, heal sickness, and even raise the dead. Of the group, Peter, James, and John formed Jesus' inner circle. They were the ones who ascended Mount Tabor just to the east of Nazareth, where they witnessed Jesus transfigured in a blaze of light. And just prior to his arrest, the three accompanied him to the garden where he prayed for guidance. ■

Jesus not only was able to feed the multitude with fish but also taught his apostles to fish for souls.

THE STORY OF MARY

THE CRUCIFIXION

~~~

During his ministry, Jesus had reached many people throughout Judea, Galilee, Samaria, and Decapolis. He realized, though, that he needed to take his message to the heart of the land. So Jesus left Galilee in 30 C.E. and traveled to Jerusalem for the festival of Passover. Mary was probably there too, because she would soon be present at the Crucifixion.

Thousands had flocked to the Temple to celebrate Passover, the holiday that recalls when the Jews were slaves to Pharaoh and Moses brought them out of Egypt to freedom. A festival praising those who challenged a great power, though, made the Romans nervous. Soldiers were on high alert to watch for trouble and agitation, and the trip filled the apostles with understandable apprehension.

MERCHANTS AND MONEY CHANGERS

Jesus needed to be seen as he arrived, and his disciples found a donkey to carry him during his jubilant entrance into Jerusalem. As he rode into the city, festival-goers spread their clothes as well as branches in his path, praising the man they heard so much about and shouting, "Hosanna!" (John 12:13). But when Jesus arrived at the Temple forecourt, he came upon a market filled with merchants selling oxen, sheep, and doves for ritual sacrifices, as well as tables set up for exchanging money. The sight horrified him, and Jesus fashioned some ropes to form a whip and drove them out. As he did, he admonished the crowd, paraphrasing the prophet Jeremiah by accusing those there of turning the sacred spot into "a den of thieves" (Matthew 21:13).

> THE CITY WAS PACKED, AND JUST AS WHEN JOSEPH AND MARY HEADED TO BETHLEHEM THREE DECADES EARLIER, ALL THE INNS WERE FULL.

The city of 40,000 residents was packed with some 180,000 people. And just as when Joseph and Mary headed down to Bethlehem three decades earlier, all the inns were full. Jesus needed a large place to accommodate his group and hold his seder—the religious meal served to commemorate the holiday—and Peter and John found for him a large room at the top of a home just to the east of the city on the Mount of Olives.

The Romans mocked Jesus before they crucified him, and pressed a crown of thorns on his head.

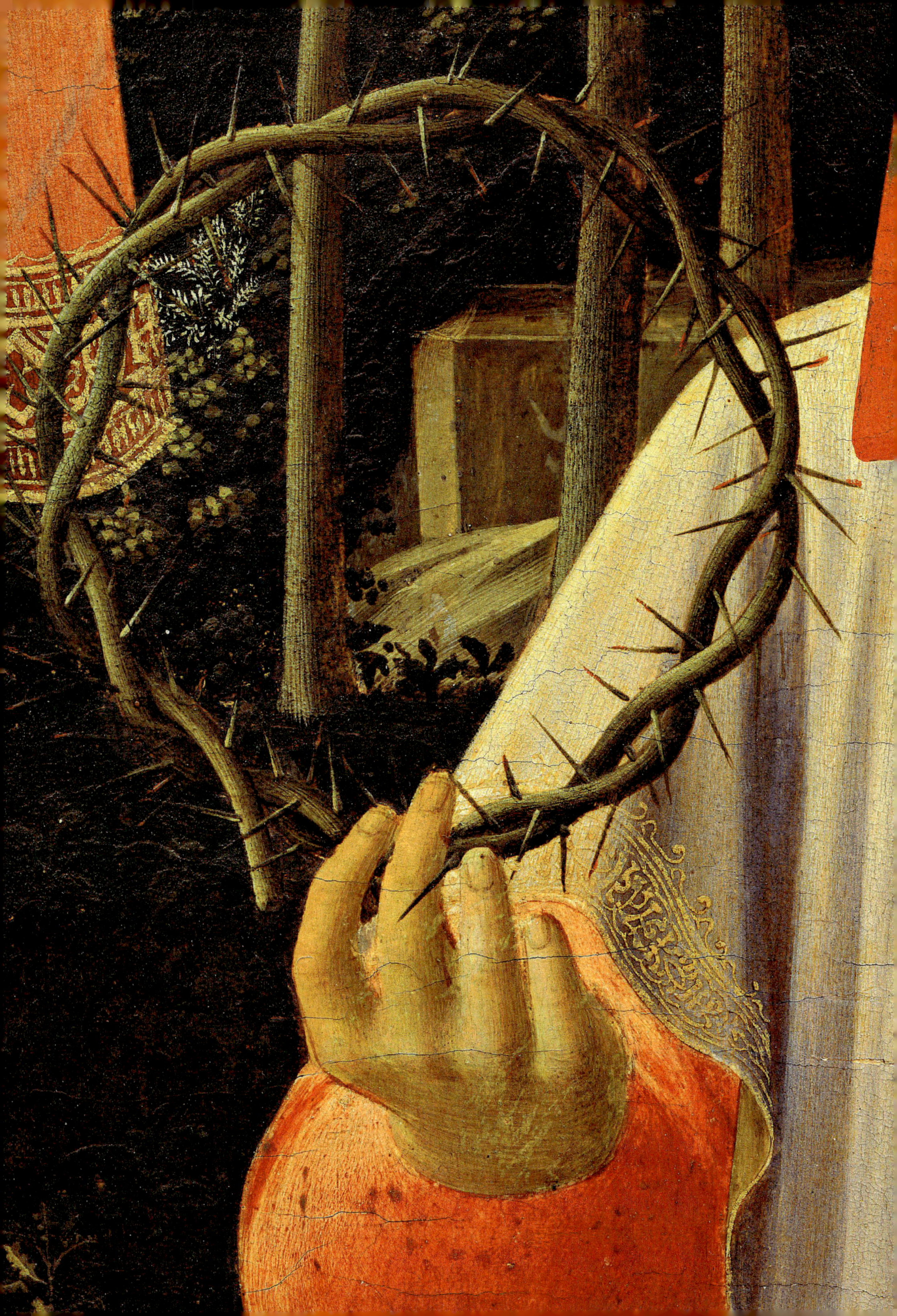

THE STORY OF MARY

THE LAST SUPPER

During the seder, the gathered would recall how God cast plague on the Egyptians—blood, frogs, bugs, wild animals, pestilence, boils, hail, locusts, and darkness—in order to convince Pharaoh to let his people

MARYAM AND MUSLIMS

In the Quran, Jesus is considered a prophet who performed miracles, and Mary, whom they call Maryam, is seen as one of the most righteous of women. She is the only woman actually named in the Quran, and the text's 19th chapter is named for her. Many Muslims visit the Tree of the Virgin Mary, a spot near Cairo where it is believed the Holy Family rested when in Egypt. And in Jerusalem, it is said that Mary washed at what is known as Mary's Bath. It has become a pilgrimage site for Muslim women who have difficulty getting pregnant.

Cairo's Virgin Mary Tree

go. Yet Pharaoh's heart remained hardened. So God told the Israelites to mark the door lintel and side post of their homes with lamb's blood so that he would know which homes to pass over as he delivered his deadliest plague: the smiting of the firstborn. Only then did Pharaoh relent and the Jews left.

For the seder, they probably would have eaten lamb. The faithful brought the animals to the Temple for the sacrifice and afterward took the carcass home to roast on a spit of pomegranate wood. As Jesus and his disciples dined, he revealed that he knew how "one of you will betray me" (Mark 14:18). He then lifted some of the matzo, the unleavened bread eaten to recall how the Israelites baked in haste when fleeing Egypt. Jesus handed out pieces and told all at the table to eat it since it represented

Roman centurions placed Jesus' cross between those of two thieves, and Mary and others gathered and watched him die.

his body. Wine is another tradition of the seder, and Jesus then raised a glass and told them to drink of it, for that represented his blood. As they did, they completed the first Eucharist, a ritual that Christians have celebrated ever since.

> **JESUS LOOKED AT HIS MOTHER AND OTHER WOMEN, SAYING, "DO NOT WEEP FOR ME; WEEP INSTEAD FOR YOURSELVES AND FOR YOUR CHILDREN."**

BLASPHEMY AND TREASON

That night, Jesus took Peter, James, and John to the Garden of Gethsemane on the east side of the Temple Mount to pray. It is here, for reasons that are unclear, that Judas betrayed him in return for 30 pieces of silver. Temple guards came and spirited Jesus to the home of Caiaphas. The Temple's high priest accused Jesus of blasphemy, hastily convicted him, and turned him over to Pontius Pilate, who served as the Roman prefect of Judea.

Pilate was staying at the praetorium, the governor's palace, during the festival. When he questioned Jesus and asked him if he was King of the Jews, Jesus responded simply, "You say so" (Luke 23:3). Such a claim was treasonous and punishable by death by crucifixion, a common form of execution for enemies of the state. It was a horrid penalty that brought on an agonizing end, during which the victim suffered from a combination of asphyxiation, reduced blood flow, and organ failure. And it was something the Romans had no reluctance to use as both a punishment and an abject warning to others. During the previous century, they had executed members of

The Gospel According to Mark reveals that Jesus was wrapped in a linen cloth and then placed in a newly carved tomb.

Spartacus's troops who fought in the gladiators' war, nailing 6,000 soldiers to crucifixes lining 130 miles of the Appian Way.

THE PLACE OF THE SKULL

The Romans whipped Jesus, dressed him in a purple robe, pushed a crown of thorns on his head, handed him a reed like a scepter, and mockingly hailed him as King of the Jews. They then marched him to Golgotha, the execution ground. As he headed to the site whose name means "place of the skull" (John 19:17), a man named Simon from Cyrene helped him carry the cross. Jesus looked at his mother and the other women following and lamenting, telling them, "Daughters of Jerusalem, do not weep for me; weep instead for yourselves and for your children" (Luke 23:28). At the execution ground, the soldiers nailed him to a crucifix, set it between the crucifixes of two criminals, and placed a sign above Jesus' head that read, "This is Jesus, the King of the Jews" (Matthew 27:37). The soldiers then drew lots to see who would get his assorted pieces of clothing and watched as he slowly died.

HER SON'S DEATH

The execution started on Friday morning. Most of his disciples had gone into hiding, and John wrote that a great multitude had gathered to witness his death. There were the centurion in charge of the sentence, soldiers, priests, elders, and members of the Sanhedrin. Most prominently, a small group of women kept vigil. These were Jesus' most faithful followers: his mother, Mary; Mary Magdalene; and his mother's sister, Mary the wife of Clopas. As Mary watched her son die a slow and painful death, he looked down at her and said, "Woman, behold, your son" (John 19:26). As darkness began to fall, Jesus then cried out, "Eli, Eli, lema sabachthani?" "My God, my God, why have you forsaken me?" (Matthew 27:46).

He then died. ■

A Greek-style necklace of the period with a rosette on the lock and a gemstone pendant on the bottom

HEROD ANTIPAS AND PONTIUS PILATE

As one of Herod the Great's surviving sons, Herod Antipas inherited part of the kingdom. He built the city of Tiberias along the Sea of Galilee and ruled during Jesus' ministry. When Jesus learned that Herod sought to kill him, he derided him as "that fox" (Luke 13:32). Herod worked with Pontius Pilate, the oppressive Roman prefect. After Jesus' arrest, Pilate sent Jesus to Antipas, who hoped that Jesus would dazzle him with some miracles. Jesus refused, and Herod sent him back to Pilate, who ordered his death.

A stone at Caesarea mentioning Pilate

THE STORY OF MARY

MARY AFTER CHRIST

Just before Jesus passed, he entrusted his mother's care to John, the only apostle present, saying to him, "Behold, your mother" (John 19:27). With his death, Jesus' broken body was lowered to the ground. One of his followers, Joseph of Arimathea, rushed off to see Pilate. He begged the leader to let him take away the body, and the prefect allowed it.

But it was Friday evening, the start of the Sabbath. Jewish law forbids burial on Saturday, so they had to wait. Joseph and Nicodemus, a Pharisee who belonged to the Sanhedrin, then wrapped Jesus in strips of linen and applied myrrh and aloes. Near where he died stood a garden with a newly carved tomb. They set Jesus inside and closed the entrance with a large stone. Fearful that one of the disciples might try to take Jesus' body, Pilate ordered guards to watch the spot.

A BURIAL GATHERING

Mark tells us that Mary Magdalene and several other women returned to the tomb on Sunday with sweet spices and ointments so they could prepare and anoint Jesus' body. But as they neared the tomb, they were stunned to discover that the huge stone had been moved. When they entered the cave, instead of finding a corpse wrapped in linen, they saw a young man seated and dressed in white. The women fell to their knees, and the man told them that Jesus was not there. He had risen, and they should go and tell the others what had happened.

Filled with both fear and joy, they ran to spread the news. Soon after, the apostles who had fled returned to Jerusalem. They gathered in the same large room where they had eaten the Last Supper.

It was a Saturday, the Sabbath, and, according to Acts, the room was filled with 120 people including Mary and Jesus' "brothers."

MATTHIAS IS CHOSEN

By then, Judas was dead. He had returned the blood silver he earned for betraying his leader. Judas either, as Matthew related, "went off and hanged himself"

THIS PAGE: **A type of lusterware vial that could have held perfumed unguents like myrrh.** OPPOSITE: **Mary, John the Evangelist, and Mary Magdalene mourning at the foot of Jesus' cross.**

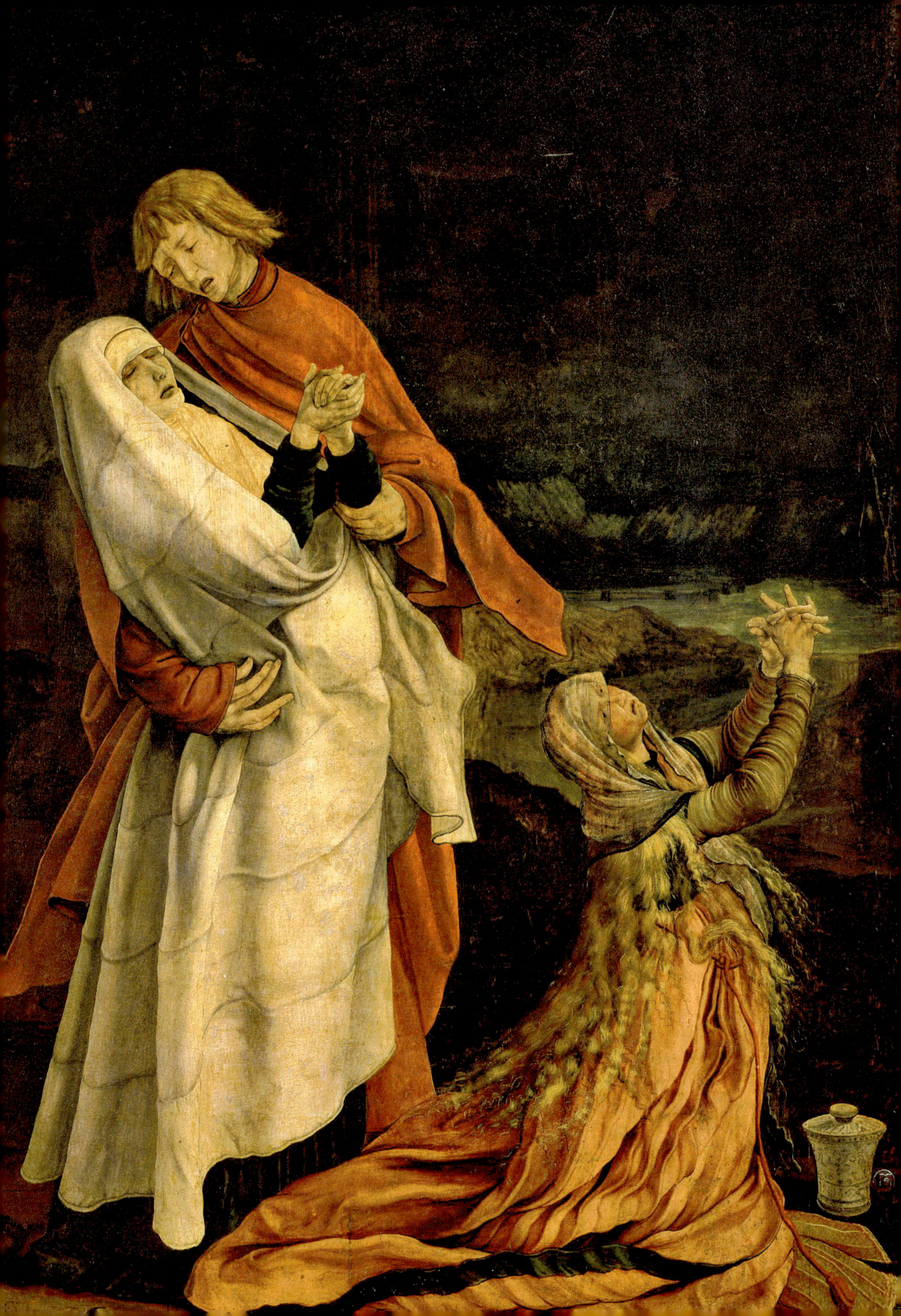

THE STORY OF MARY

Raphael's painting of the Transfiguration for Rome's St. Peter's Basilica was his last work.

(Matthew 27:5) or, as mentioned in Acts, fell over and "burst open in the middle, and all his insides spilled out" (Acts 1:18). The apostles needed someone to replace Judas to help continue spreading Jesus' message and sought a follower who had long been a part of Jesus' mission. Two men qualified, Joseph Barsabbas and Matthias. The disciples cast lots and chose Matthias, who had been with Jesus from the time of his baptism by John the Baptist.

A HARVEST GATHERING

Not long after, the apostles and followers gathered for Shavuot, the harvest festival. The holiday's name means "weeks," and it is celebrated seven weeks following Passover. For this holiday, the faithful gathered the *bikkurim,* the season's first fruits—wheat, barley, grapes, figs, pomegranates, olives, and dates—and headed to the Temple to make their offering and give thanks to God. They put the fruits in baskets with turtledoves tied to them. The rich brought containers decorated with gold and silver, and the poor, simple wicker ones. The trip to Jerusalem would have been a joyous one. On their journey, the celebrants would be led by a flute

HOUSE OF THE VIRGIN MARY

Not far from the ruins of Ephesus stands the House of the Virgin Mary. The building dates from the sixth century, although there are first-century remains below. In 1896, Pope Leo XIII blessed the site. John Paul II visited in 1979, and Benedict XVI performed a Mass there in 2006. The home attracts both the faithful and the curious. It has a spring where visitors can make a wish before tasting the water, which is claimed to have curative powers. There is also a Wishing Wall, where they can attach a possession as they make their request.

The interior of Mary's home in Ephesus, Turkey

Ruins in Ephesus, the city where Mary might have gone with John following Jesus' death

player; they would take with them an ox with an olive-crown placed on its head, its horns bedecked with gold.

THE BIRTH OF THE CHURCH

The disciples had gotten together in an upper room to celebrate the holiday. Suddenly they heard a noise coming from heaven like that of a mighty rushing wind, and it filled the house. The Book of Acts reveals that the Holy Spirit came down and filled all who were there. Inspired to tell others the good news, Peter told them to spread the word that Jesus was

> **FOR THIS HOLIDAY, THE FAITHFUL GATHERED THE *BIKKURIM*, THE SEASON'S FIRST FRUITS, AND HEADED TO THE TEMPLE TO MAKE THEIR OFFERING.**

made by God and exhorted all to "repent and be baptized" and to "save yourselves from this corrupt generation" (Acts 2:38-40). That day, 3,000 people took the rites. Christians have since celebrated this day as Pentecost, which in Greek means "50th," and see it as the day that the church was born. ■

THE STORY OF MARY

MARY'S DEATH AND ASSUMPTION

Mary would have been nearing 50 years old when Jesus died, but there's no solid record on where she went after his death. It seems from her presence in the upper room following the Crucifixion that she was around for the early days of what would become Jesus' church. It is possible that she stayed in Jerusalem or spent time back at her home in Nazareth.

She would have had a community of people to care for her. One who might have helped was the apostle James. Also known as James the Just, he is referred to in the Gospels as one of Jesus' four brothers and as the Lord's Brother. Whether he was a brother or possibly a stepbrother or cousin, James could be considered family and might have watched over Mary. The Epistle of James has been attributed to him, and he, along with Peter and John the Evangelist, became prominent leaders in building the Jerusalem church and spreading Jesus' message.

JEWISH LAW AND THE GENTILES

As the church grew, its leaders in 48 C.E. held the Council of Jerusalem. Jesus' followers were Jews and still considered themselves Jewish. But with more gentiles joining the fold, the council considered what requirements of Jewish law the new church's followers had to obey. While it was decided that men did not have to be circumcised, the council accepted James's insistence that other tenets be maintained: Those who joined could not worship other gods, eat foods prepared improperly, eat blood, and take part in illicit sexual activity.

A PEACEFUL DEATH

And just as we don't know when Mary died, there are no writings covering her death. Based on later writings, the Eastern Orthodox and the Catholic Church hold that she was assumed, body and soul, into heaven. Catholics believe that she was alive when taken into heaven, while the Orthodox believe she died a natural death and her body was then taken up. At the base of the

THIS PAGE: **A terra-cotta figurine of a mother and child.** OPPOSITE: **Giovanni Battista Tiepolo's vision of Mary's Assumption.**

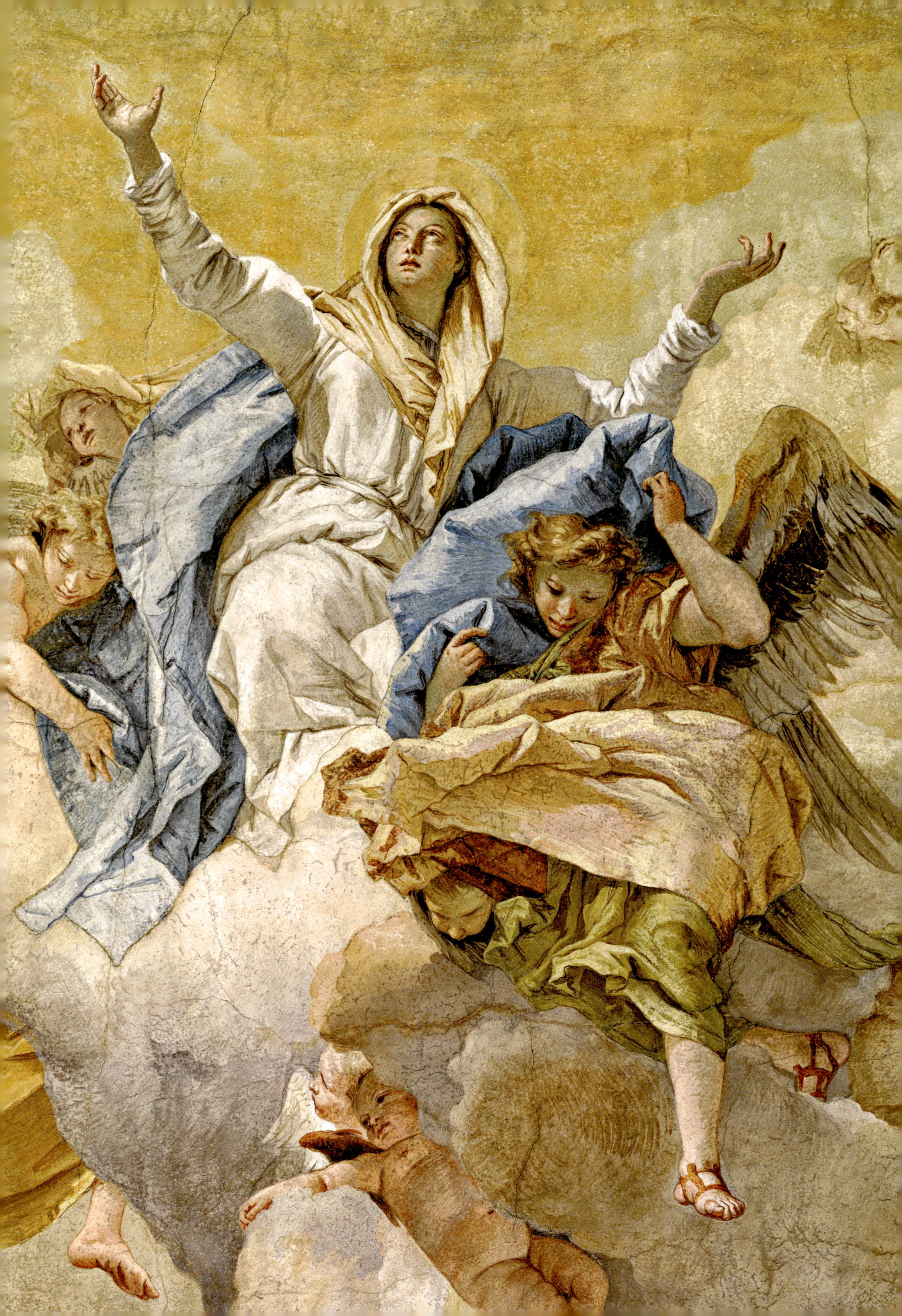

THE STORY OF MARY

"THE ONLY APOSTLE WHO DOES NOT SEEM TO HAVE SUFFERED A VIOLENT DEATH WAS JOHN, WHOM JESUS ENTRUSTED WITH MARY'S CARE.

AACHEN CATHEDRAL

The Aachen Cathedral in Germany claims Mary's cloak and the swaddling clothes she placed on the infant Jesus, the loincloth he wore on the cross, and the cloth on which John the Baptist's head was set. All are housed in the Marienschrein, the Shrine of Saint Mary. This gemstone-encrusted golden reliquary from the 13th century is shaped like an ornate cruciform and decorated with images of Jesus, Mary, and the apostles. In the 14th century, the church began to display the four sacred relics about every seven years.

The Aachen Cathedral holds numerous relics.

Mount of Olives stands the Tomb of the Virgin Mary, the spot where it is said that her body last existed on earth before she went to heaven. It is both a Christian shrine and also visited by Muslims who likewise revere her.

THE APOSTLES' END

While Mary was said to have peacefully gone to heaven, many early church leaders faced severe persecution. James the Greater was the first of the apostles to die, with the Book of Acts saying that Herod Agrippa had him killed with a sword. Jesus' "brother" James the Just was said to have been tossed from the Temple parapet and then stoned and beaten to death. Peter is reported to have been crucified upside down in Rome. Andrew was crucified on an X-shaped cross, which became known as the St. Andrew's Cross. Philip either died of old age or was crucified in what is now Turkey. Bartholomew was killed in Armenia. Thomas reportedly was martyred while in India. Matthew died by beheading or stoning. Thaddaeus, otherwise known as Jude, was killed in Beirut. And Simon was sliced in half in Persia.

The only apostle who does not seem to have suffered a violent death was John, whom Jesus entrusted with Mary's care and who spent time in Ephesus in present-day Turkey. So though there is a tomb for Mary in Jerusalem, there is the belief that she might have traveled to Ephesus. The city had an early Christian community, and Mary is said to have lived nearby in a small cottage. In the fifth century, the faithful built the Church of Mary, thought to be the first church dedicated to her.

MARY'S HOME

In the early 19th century, Anne Catherine Emmerich, an Augustinian nun, received visions of Mary and her home. In 1881, a priest who read Emmerich's account searched for the house and found a small stone home overlooking the Aegean that matched her description. Soon after, two missionaries also searched for and found the same building. The spot, it was learned, had long been revered in Turkey as the Doorway to the Holy Virgin, where pilgrims celebrated the Feast of the Assumption. ■

The apostles mourn the passing of Mary in this 17th-century painting by Caravaggio.

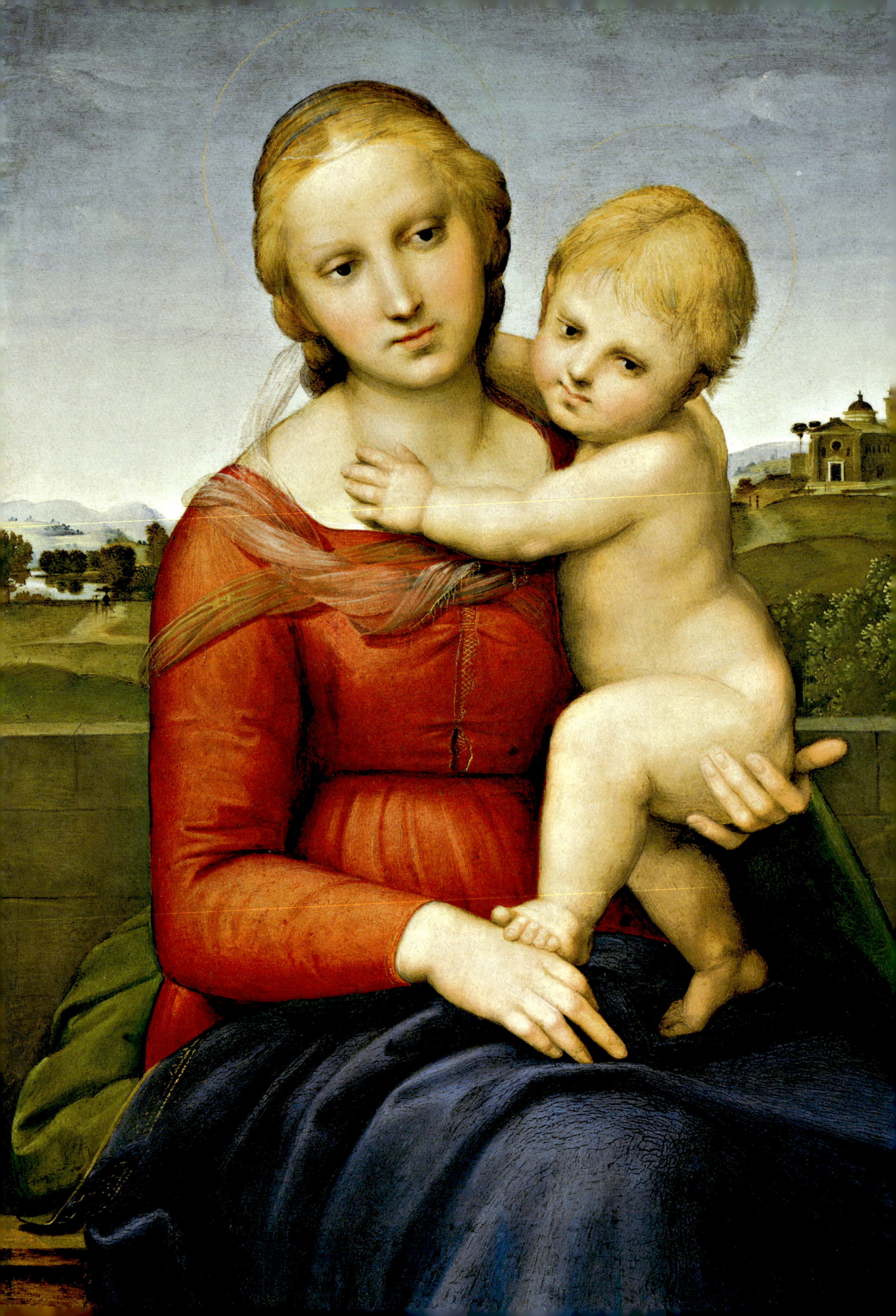

CHAPTER 4

Saint Mary
AN EXALTED, UNIQUE VENERATION

Mary was a young Jewish girl from Nazareth, a small community where nothing of note ever seemed to happen. She could never have fathomed that God would choose her. Yet when the Angel Gabriel revealed her fate, she willingly did as asked because of loving devotion to the Lord.

But Mary could not have foreseen her child's future, his ministry and miracles, his agonizing death and the glorious Resurrection. Throughout, Mary cared for, followed, and loved her son. To such a woman is owed special respect, and many have elevated her above all other humans. She is seen as the seminal mother, the nurturing parent, the patient guardian, the paragon of virtue, the symbol of human sacrifice, suffering, and love.

Mary is the great Mediatrix, the mediator between humans and Christ, first witnessed during the Wedding at Cana. The celebration ran out of wine, and Mary quickly interceded by encouraging her son to help. Her presence and patience has been celebrated in paintings, sculptures, stained glass windows, music, and cathedrals.

The Catholic Church accords *cultus latria,* adoration, solely to God. Saints and angels receive a form of veneration called *cultus dulia.* Mary, though, has earned *hyperdulia,* the highest form of veneration as the holiest of creatures. Even so, the church has long wrestled with how to fully honor her, and over the past 16 centuries it has approved four dogmas: the belief in the Theotokos, that Mary is the Mother of God; the Immaculate Conception; the Assumption into Heaven; and her Perpetual Virginity.

ABOVE: **A terra-cotta figure from the first century.** OPPOSITE: **Raphael's portrait of the Madonna and child was painted by the Urbino artist when he was 22 and reveals Leonardo's influence.**

THE STORY OF MARY

THE COUNCIL OF EPHESUS

As the church struggled with forming the nascent religion, it needed to tackle thorny ecumenical issues, as well as how to define Mary, and it started holding councils to resolve differences within its growing parts. In 325, a council under Pope Sylvester I and Emperor Constantine condemned the idea of Arianism: the belief that if God created Jesus, then Jesus was a demigod.

The question of who or what was Mary also proved contentious. Could she be—as Nestorius, bishop of Constantinople believed—a *Christotokos,* a "Christ-bearer," the mother who gave birth to a human who became God? Or was she—as Cyril, the bishop of Alexandria, along with Pope Celestine I and others insisted—*Theotokos,* the Mother of God? If so, Jesus was not only God's son but also born God and therefore encompasses two natures: the human and the divine.

In 431, 250 bishops gathered in Ephesus to resolve Mary's position as well as Jesus' divine nature. Though Nestorius attacked the idea of giving Mary the title *Theotokos,* Cyril was determined to have his belief accepted. Believing Nestorius's ideas smacked of heresy, Cyril started the proceedings before he arrived. By the time the council ended, a parade left the church proclaiming Mary the Theotokos. The church then removed Nestorius from office.

A first-century B.C.E. clay oil lamp gave off a soft light.

Ephesus was also the home of the Temple of Artemis. This Greek structure was dedicated to Zeus and Leto's daughter, goddess of the hunt, fertility, and birth and guardian of young children. She was worshipped throughout Greece and Turkey. Not surprisingly, the city became home to her fertility cult.

Artemis's cult of the Theotokos caused conflict with members of the developing church. John and Paul arrived in Ephesus in the first century when the worship of the goddess proved strong, and Paul's active and aggressive missionary work upset the locals. The Book of Acts tells of a silversmith named Demetrius who made a good living fashioning silver shrines for the goddess. The artisan complained to his fellow craftsmen that Paul's conversions were costing all of them business, that Paul "has persuaded and misled a great number of people by saying that gods made by hands are not gods at all" (Acts 19:26). A large and unruly crowd then gathered to protest the Christians, shouting,

"Great is Artemis of the Ephesians!" (Acts 19:28). Paul wanted to confront the group, but his followers advised him against it, and he soon left for Macedonia.

SHRINES TO THE VIRGIN

The invading Goths destroyed Artemis's temple in 268 C.E., and because of John and Paul's work, the area became a major Christian center. Soon a church rose within the remains of a second-century Roman cultural center. The space was eventually split in two: one dedicated to Mary, the other to St. John the Evangelist. This gave the double church its name: Holiest Church of the Most Holy, Most Honoured and Eternal Virgin Mary. It is the first of seven churches mentioned in the Book of Revelation; the others are Smyrna, Pergamum, Thyatira, Sardis, Philadelphia, and Laodicea.

With the Ephesus council, Pope Sixtus III decided to build his shrine to Mary closer to home. Constructed between 432 and 440, the Basilica of Santa Maria Maggiore is Rome's largest Marian church, and its interior includes a triumphal arch with glowing mosaics showing the Annunciation, Joseph's dream, and the Adoration of the Magi. In 1931, on the 1,500th anniversary of the 431 council, Pope Pius XI set October 11 as the Feast of the Divine Maternity of Our Lady. ∎

The Magi appeared in Bethlehem, marveled at Jesus' birth, and brought him precious gifts.

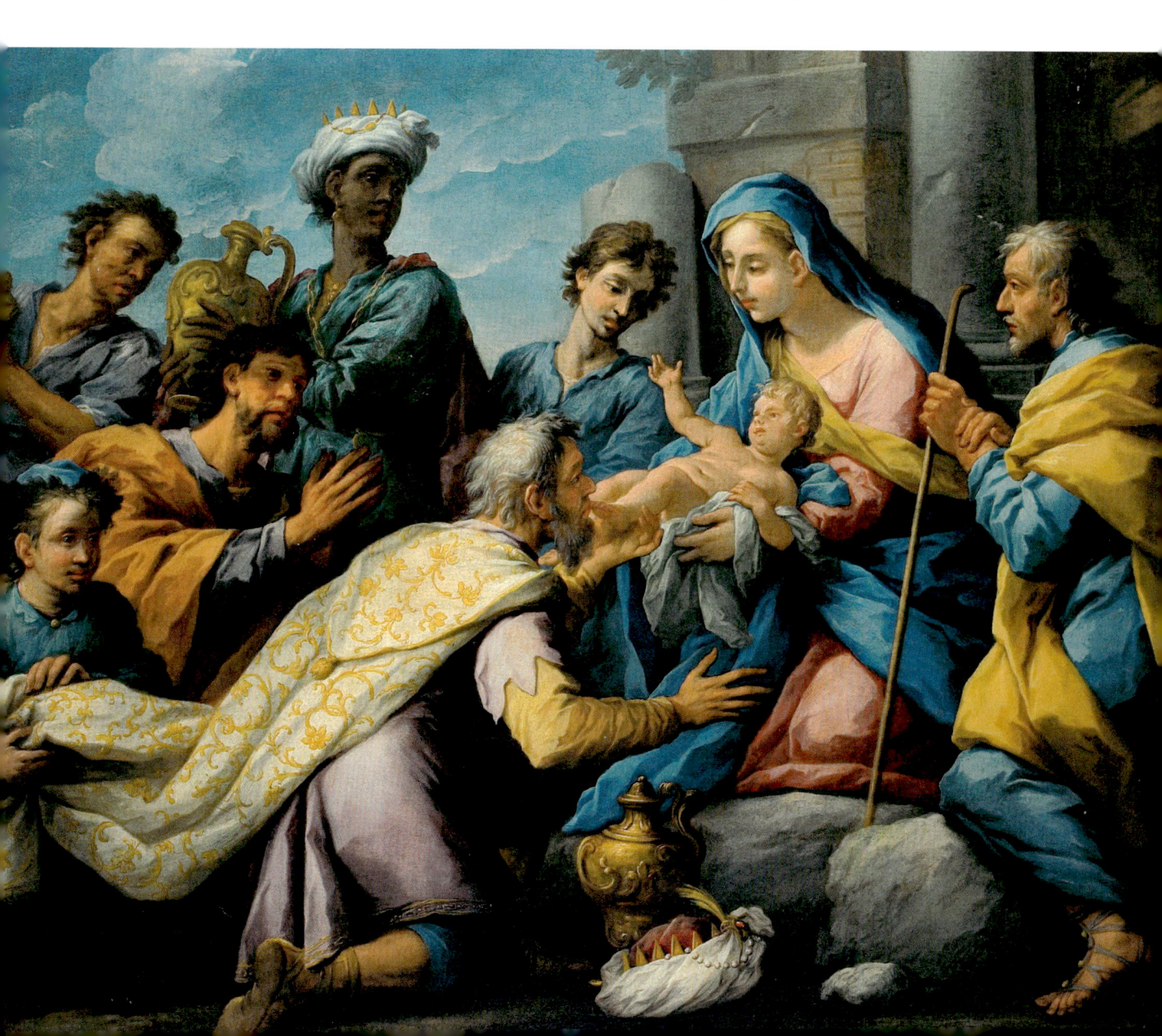

THE COUNCIL OF LATERAN

The Gospels mention other children in Mary's household, with Matthew noting how during one of Jesus' visits to a synagogue in Nazareth someone voices his amazement at Jesus' knowledge and comments, "Is he not the carpenter's son? Is not his mother named Mary and his brothers James, Joseph, Simon, and Judas? Are not his sisters all with us?" (Matthew 13:55-56).

While the Protestant reformer Martin Luther stated, "It is an article of faith that Mary is Mother of the Lord and still a virgin," many Protestants believe that there were "brethren of the lord" and that Mary had children following Jesus' birth. This idea that Jesus had siblings and possibly older brothers goes against the basic belief that Mary was a virgin at the time of his conception.

Yet Catholic theologians have long stressed that these children were either Joseph's from his previous marriage or Jesus' cousins within their household. As Elaine Pagels, professor of religion at Princeton University, notes, "The Catholic Church later called them cousins because they thought it was a little inappropriate for a virgin to be having older children before she had Jesus."

FAMILY EXTENSIONS

The second-century Apocrypha volume, the Protoevangelium of James, discusses this extended family by stating that Joseph was an older widower with children. After he was chosen as Mary's husband during a ceremony at the Temple, the priests entrusted Joseph with the care of "keeping the virgin of the Lord." Part of believers' defense also rests on the loose definition of the term *brother* in the Bible.

In Genesis, Lot, the nephew of Abraham whose wife "looked back" (Genesis 19:26) and turned to a pillar of salt, is first described in some translations as Abraham's brother's son. But just two sentences later, he is called his brother.

SCRIPTURE VERSUS BELIEF

At the start of the Gospel According to Matthew, after Joseph is told not to abandon Mary, the book states: "He had no

THIS PAGE: **A luminous German, 13th-century stained glass window showing the Holy Family fleeing for Egypt.** OPPOSITE: **Raphael's "Virgin of the Rose, Madonna and Child With Joseph and John the Baptist."**

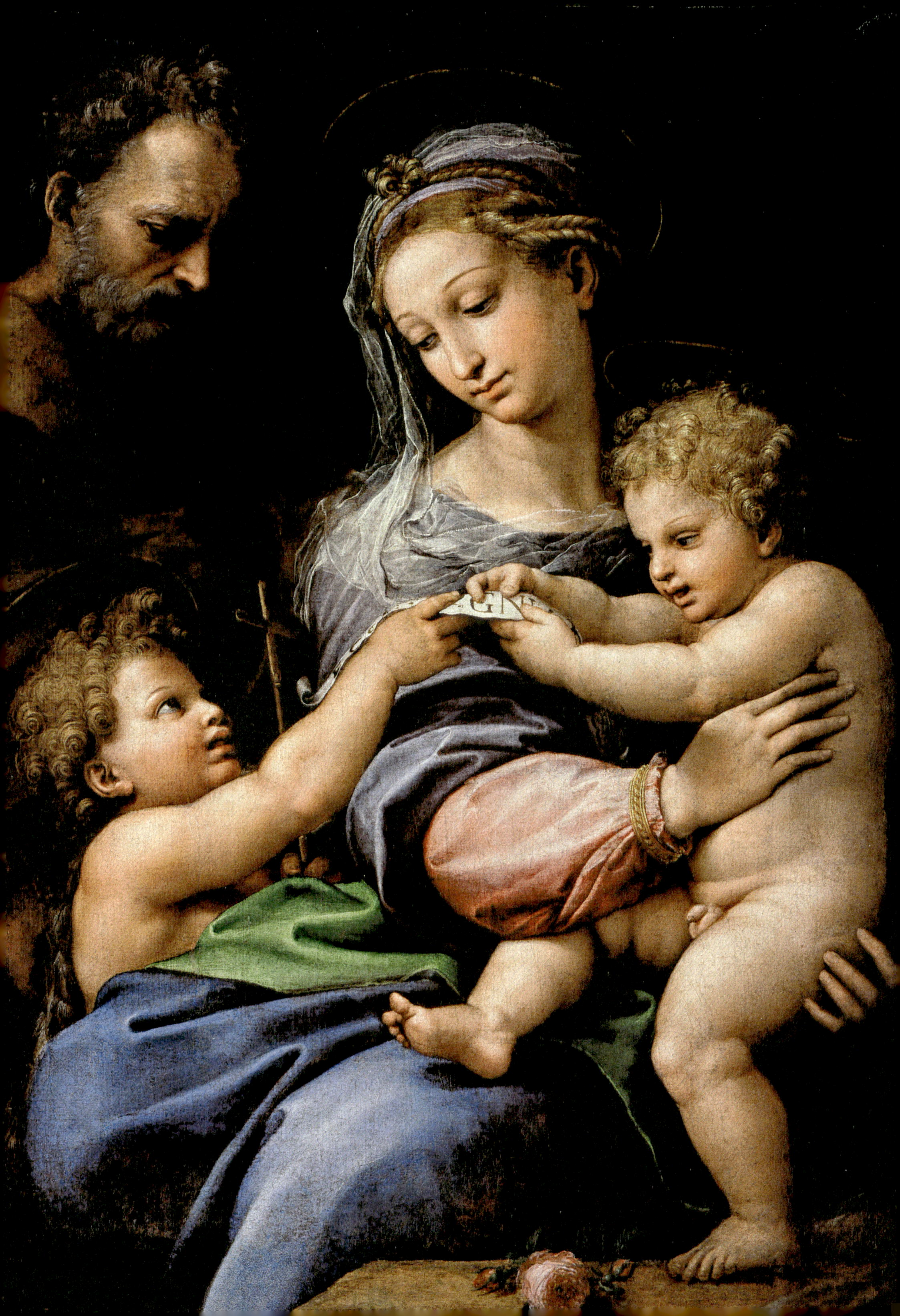

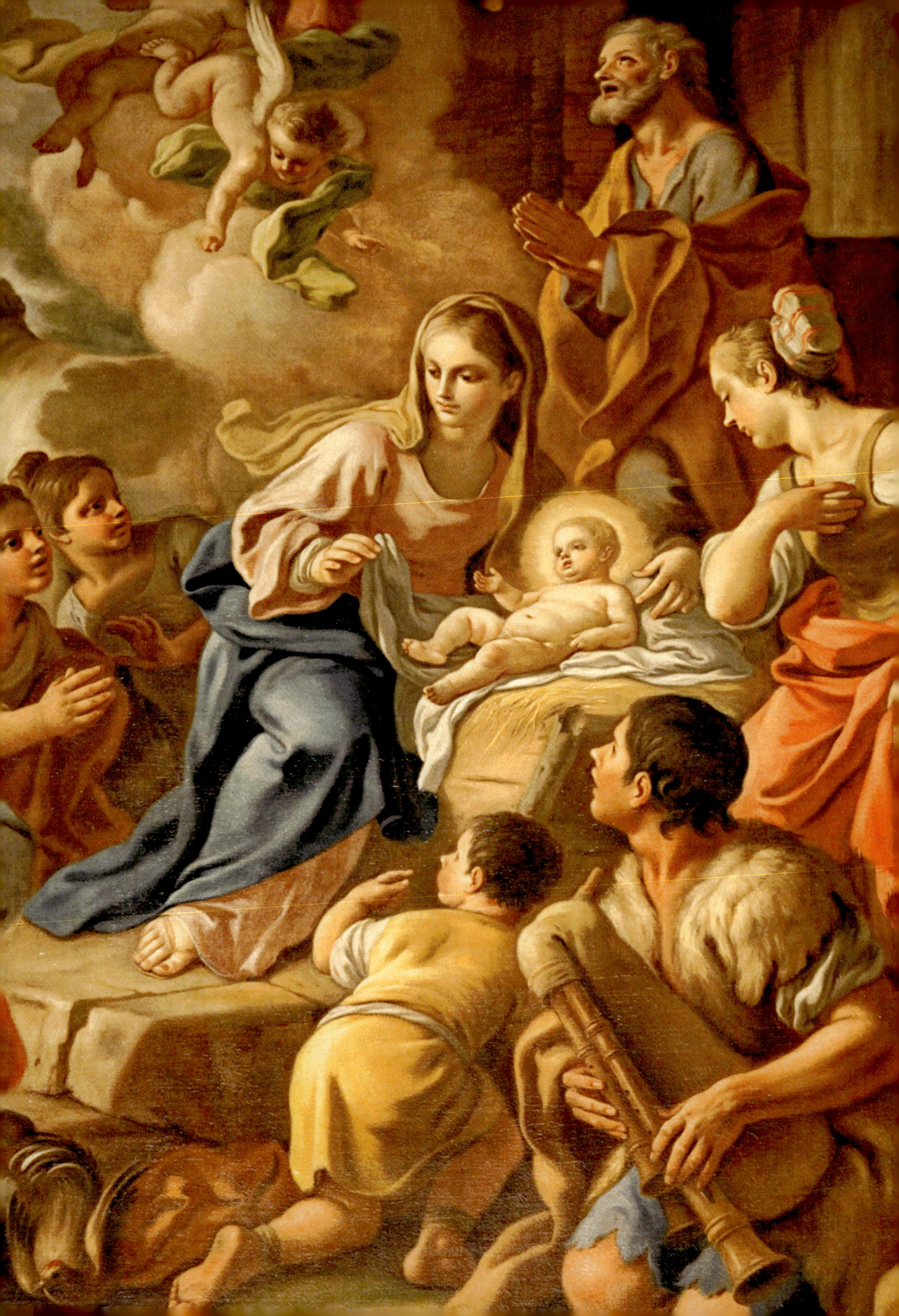

relations with her until she bore a son" (Matthew 1:25). Some also see this as proof that the couple soon after consummated their union and would have then had other children. In response, defenders of Mary's virginity point out that some translations that say he "knew her not" was just an idiomatic expression and that the term *firstborn* means only that she gave birth when she never had before. They indicate as proof the passage in Exodus (13:2) where God tells Moses, "Consecrate to me every firstborn."

Throughout the centuries, the Catholic Church has held that Jesus was not only uniquely conceived with the aid of the Holy Spirit, but that Mary was a virgin before the Angel Gabriel's visit and stayed that way after her child arrived. In October 649, a council of 105 bishops gathered at Rome's Lateran Church. There, under the watchful eye of Pope Martin I, the council got to work and presented 20 canons.

One of the canons holds that Mary was a virgin before, during, and after Jesus' birth. "If anyone does not, in accord with the Holy Fathers, acknowledge the holy and ever virgin and immaculate Mary as really and truly the Mother of God," the council intoned for those who might question their finding, "inasmuch as she, in the fullness of time and without human seed, conceived by the Holy Spirit God the Word Himself, who before all time was born of God the Father; and without loss of her integrity, brought Him forth; and after His birth preserved her virginity inviolate, let him be condemned."

THIS PAGE: **"The Adoration of the Magi"** in the Uffizi Gallery, Florence. OPPOSITE: **"The Adoration of the Shepherds"** in San Nicola alla Carità church, Naples, Italy.

EVER VIRGIN

In the 1960s, Vatican II reaffirmed the idea, stating that Mary was an Ever-Virgin. The 16th Centenary of the Plenary Council of Capua near Naples discussed Mary's Perpetual Virginity. At the end of the 1992 conference, Pope John Paul II said, "The Church proclaims as factually true that Mary . . . truly and virginally gave birth to her Son, for Whom she remained a virgin after birth; a virgin—according to the holy Fathers and Councils which expressly dealt with the question." ∎

> "AFTER JOSEPH IS TOLD NOT TO ABANDON MARY, MATTHEW STATES: "HE HAD NO RELATIONS WITH HER UNTIL SHE BORE A SON.""

THE IMMACULATE CONCEPTION

The story of Mary starts before her birth. Only a woman who is pure could be the mother of God. But to be pure meant to be free from original sin, the taint attached to all humans after Adam and Eve fell from grace when they ate from the Tree of Life. To ensure Mary's sinlessness, the womb of her mother, Anne, was said to have been shielded before Mary was conceived.

Although numerous texts in both the Bible and the New Testament are used to defend the idea of the Immaculate Conception, it does not appear in the Gospels. Instead, the concept evolved from nonbiblical tradition during the early days of the Church. As Jesus' mother, the belief holds, Mary had a special holiness, a quality that would be affirmed when the bishops met in Ephesus and declared her Theotokos. Because she was the Mother of God, it made sense that someone so near to God could not possess sinful attributes.

This idea that she was spared from sin was spelled out by the 13th-century philosopher John Duns Scotus. His Marian defense spread and became promoted by such popes as Sixtus IV, who in 1476 instituted the Feast of the Immaculate Conception. Mary's special quality was also recognized by the Council of Basel in the 1430s and the Council of Trent. That ecumenical meeting spanned from 1545 to 1563 and was a response to the seismic shifts brought on by the Reformation and the Catholic Church's need to renew itself. The council issued many decrees, such as eliminating the abuse of indulgences and defining the doctrines that Protestants objected to.

This Counter-Reformation ultimately revitalized the church. Yet throughout, many Catholics held tightly to their beliefs. One of the faithful, Catherine Labouré, had joined the Daughters of Charity in Paris as a novice in 1830. That year, she experienced visions of Mary while at her convent of Rue du Bac. In one, she saw a picture of the virgin standing on a globe. With her were the words, "Mary conceived without sin, pray for us who have recourse to thee." On the opposite side of the image appeared a cross, two hearts, 12 stars, and the letter M. After the archbishop learned of Labouré's vision, he had thousands of medallions minted with the image and words. Soon after, the Jesuit professor Giovanni Perrone wrote that while no scriptural writings support the idea of the Immaculate Conception, none say it is untrue either.

Greek-style hairpins that were popular in the Holy Land at the time of the Roman occupation

An 18th-century painting attributed to Francesco Solimena that portrays the Immaculate Conception

A DOCTRINE PROCLAIMED

Hoping to resolve the issue of the Immaculate Conception, Pope Pius IX asked the church's bishops for their thoughts. A majority agreed it was true. Then in 1854 in the *Ineffabilis Deus,* Mary's Immaculate Conception became dogma. In front of 170 bishops and countless pilgrims, Pius declared "that the doctrine which holds that the Blessed Virgin Mary, at the first instant of her conception, by a singular privilege and grace of the Omnipotent God, in virtue of the merits of Jesus Christ, the Savior of mankind, was preserved immaculate from all stain of original sin, has been revealed by God, and therefore should firmly and constantly be believed by all the faithful."

The church canonized Labouré in 1947 as it extolled Mary. In 1986, Pope John Paul II said, "Mary, at the side of her Son, is the most perfect image of freedom and of the liberation of humanity and of the universe. It is to her, as Mother and Model, that the Church must look in order to understand in its completeness the meaning of her own mission." Seven years later, he beatified the philosopher Scotus. ■

THE STORY OF MARY

THE ASSUMPTION

By the mid-20th century, World Wars I and II had taken the lives of more than 70 million people, destroyed societies, toppled nations, and crushed the faith of countless parishioners. The church needed to help people understand that there was still much meaning on the planet. To do this, Pope Pius XII declared a dogma for Mary's assumption into heaven.

As with the Immaculate Conception, there is no mention of the Assumption in the Gospels. Other texts were therefore cited to prove the point. The idea of Mary's assumption dates from around the fourth century, when there was a growing interest in her life and death and a tendency in the early years of the church to describe Mary's life in ways not different from how they viewed Jesus'.

MARY'S PASSING

The fourth-century apocryphal work *Transitus Virginis (The Passing of the Virgin)* discussed Mary's death. It states that the apostles all gathered around Mary's deathbed, and Jesus and the angels descended from heaven and took her soul. The apostles then set Mary in a tomb. After three days, Jesus visited her burial site, when he returned her soul to her body and brought her, alive, into heaven.

There are a number of tales of Thomas's presence at the Assumption that also have parallels to what the Gospels say about Jesus' death and resurrection. One states that Thomas arrived late for her funeral, and when her tomb was opened, it was empty. Another story has Thomas showing up only as Mary is being raised into heaven. She drops to him her cincture, her belt, as proof that it was her.

By the fifth century, as belief in Mary's assumption spread, some areas celebrated Mary's passing in the Dormition of Our Lady, a feast that recognized her death and spiriting straight to heaven. Then in the late sixth century, St. Gregory of Tours wrote that in Mary's final days, "The course of this life having been completed by the Blessed Mary . . . [the Lord] commanded that [her holy body] be taken in a cloud into paradise." And in the eighth century,

THIS PAGE: **A golden vase.** OPPOSITE: **A detail of Titian's early 16th-century portrayal of "Assumption of the Virgin."**

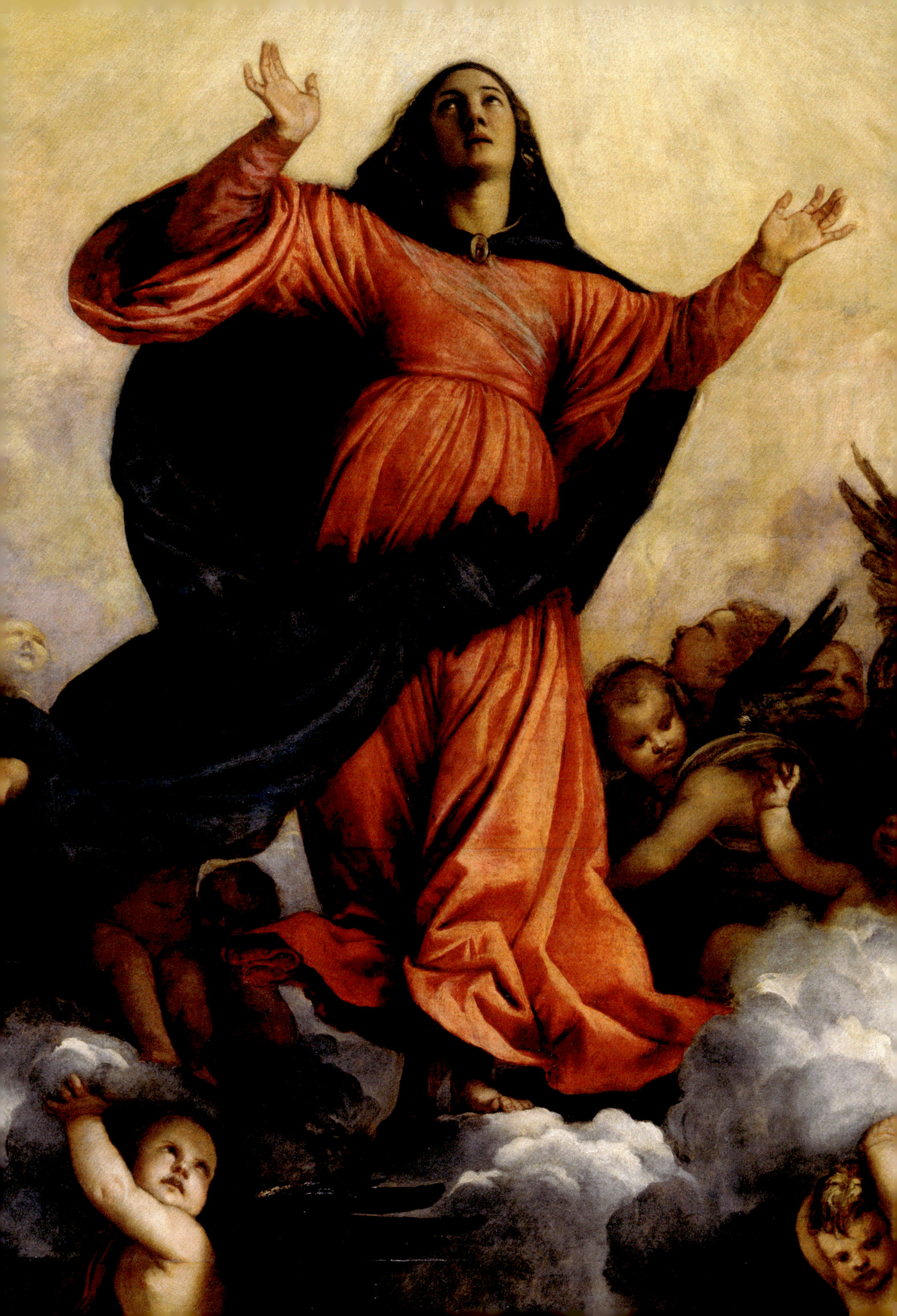

THE STORY OF MARY

Since ORIGINAL SIN *had not stained* MARY'S SOUL,
it seemed logical to worshippers to believe her body
COULD NOT BE CORRUPTED BY DEATH.

MARY'S BELT

Both Catholic and Orthodox Churches hold that Mary was assumed to heaven, with Catholics believing this happened while she was alive and the Orthodox, right after her death. According to Catholic belief, as Mary rose toward the clouds, she presented her camel-hair belt to the apostle Thomas, who had just rushed back from his mission in India to attend to her. Called the *Sacra Cintola*, it is kept in a reliquary at Tuscany's Prato Cathedral. Five times a year, including on Mary's birthday on September 8, it is taken out.

The church in Prato has Mary's belt.

St. John Damascene wrote that God "was pleased even after [Mary's] departure from life to honor her immaculate and undefiled body with incorruption and with translation [Assumption] prior to the common and universal resurrection." At that time, Pope Sergius brought the Dormition of Our Lady feast to Rome; Pope Hadrian soon renamed it the Assumption of St. Mary.

MARY'S VISITATIONS

During the Middle Ages, the topic of the Assumption appeared in artwork, showing angels lifting Mary into heaven as the apostles gaze in awe. It also proved popular on Renaissance and Baroque-era altarpieces. As reports of visitations by Mary increased in the 19th and early 20th centuries—such as Catherine Labouré's encounter in Paris, Bernadette Soubirous's in Lourdes, and Francisco Marto, Jacinta Marto, and Lucia Dos Santos's sightings in Fatima, Portugal—the church needed to address her assumption. Since it had been established that original sin had not stained Mary's soul, it seemed logical to worshippers to believe her body could not be corrupted by death.

A POPULAR BELIEF

Many Catholics had written to the Vatican about this, with the Holy See receiving more than 2,500 petitions from bishops and superiors of religious orders. Eight million letters from parishioners also arrived voicing their belief in Mary's Assumption. In 1946, Pius XII sent out *Deiparae Virginis Mariae,* an encyclical letter, to learn what bishops, the clergy, and congregants thought about such a dogma. In the responses, some 1,200 bishops agreed that the Assumption had happened, while fewer than two dozen did not.

In 1950, Rome hosted the Eighth International Marian Congress. The day after it closed, November 1, All Saints Day, Pius made a proclamation in the Piazza of St. Peter's in front of 40 cardinals, 500 bishops, and one million others: "That the Immaculate Mother of God, the ever-virgin Mary, having completed the course of her earthly life, was assumed body and soul into heavenly glory."

Correggio's murals in the Duomo of Parma offer a vivid vision of Mary's glorious assumption to heaven.

THE STORY OF MARY

DEVOTION TO MARY

There is a long, rich tradition of people and groups devoted to Mary. As the mother of God and the great intercessor, she helps bring about miracles. Because of this, millions of the faithful pray to her and make their way to her shrines, which are found around the world in the Netherlands, Rwanda, South Korea, Bosnia, Algeria, and Sri Lanka, among other places.

Martin Luther, who set off the Protestant Reformation in 1517, believed that Mary was a paragon of faithfulness. Yet while Protestants respect Mary as the mother of Jesus, they subscribe to the understanding that since there is little written about her in the Gospels, veneration of her can be seen as excessive. Even so, there have been recent ecumenical discussions between the Catholic and Anglican Church on the position of Mary.

DEDICATION TO THE VIRGIN

The Roman Church has a long and storied history of Marian groups. In 1563, Jesuit Father John Leunis was teaching in Belgium and persuaded his students to dedicate themselves to the Virgin. The group, which called itself the Sodality of Our Lady, spread across Europe, its followers giving themselves over to prayer and service to the poor. The group, whose members included the Flemish painter Peter Paul Rubens, also dedicated itself to staging short plays and holding debates on religion.

In 1673, a Roman Catholic priest named Stanislaus Papczyński founded the Marians of the Immaculate Conception. The Polish group worked to promote Mary's message of mercy. Taking a lesson from the Virgin—who had compassion for sinners and as a mediator between humanity and God could bestow the Lord's mercy—the group prayed for souls suffering in purgatory. Heavily persecuted prior to the 1917 Russian Revolution, the Marians of the Immaculate Conception soon spread throughout some 20 countries from the United States and the United Kingdom to Argentina, Belarus, Kazakhstan,

> **AS THE SODALITY OF OUR LADY SPREAD ACROSS EUROPE, ITS FOLLOWERS GAVE THEMSELVES OVER TO PRAYER AND SERVICE TO THE POOR.**

Worshippers pray in Fatima, Portugal, where once three young shepherds were greeted by Mary.

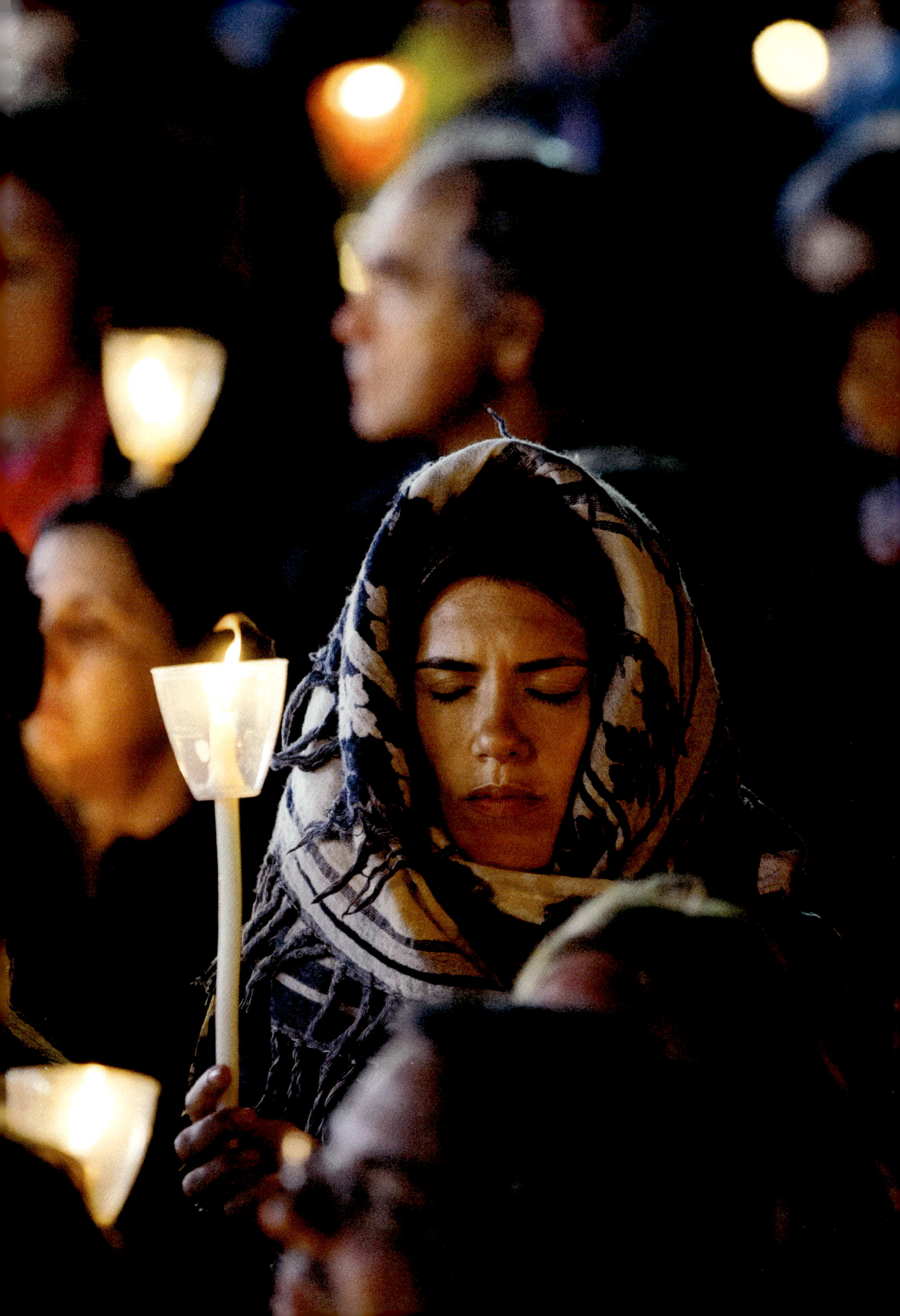

Cameroon, Rwanda, the Philippines, and Ukraine. Today, the organization prints and distributes pamphlets, prayer cards, books, and images; runs street ministries; builds schools; and distributes food and clothing.

THE GRAPEVINE CROSS

According to legend, Mary appeared to Nino of Cappadocia in present-day Turkey when she was asleep. As the Turkish woman dreamed, Mary presented Nino with the Grapevine Cross and told her to go and preach the gospel, saying, "Receive this cross as a shield against visible and invisible enemies!" When Nino awoke, she found the cross in her hands. She then traveled to Georgia and helped found the church there. The cross has since become a major symbol of the Georgian Orthodox Church and is housed in Tbilisi's Sioni Cathedral.

The cathedral in Tbilisi, Georgia

THE MARIAN MOVEMENT SPREADS

The Marist Brothers started in 1816 when 12 young men about to be ordained priests in Lyons, France, trekked up the steep hill to the shrine of Our Lady and there pledged their lives to the service of others. They all felt called to a life of compassion and mercy, in which they would reflect "the face of Mary." The group came to the United States during the Civil War to tend to French-speaking minorities in Louisiana, Maine, Massachusetts, Minnesota, and California. They opened a school in Georgia and undertook missions to the rural poor. Its members continue to fight for the poor and seek better working conditions and pay for them.

Friar William Joseph Chaminade founded the Marianists in France in 1817. Also known as the Society of Mary, the group worked to repair damage done to the church during the French Revolution when religion was repressed. The Marianists first spread to Switzerland, then to Austria and Italy, and eventually to North America, the Hawaiian Islands, Spain, Japan,

Cosmas Damian Asam's heavenly frescoes hover over the pews at the Asam Church Maria de Victoria in Ingolstadt, Germany.

In May 2017 Pope Francis performed a Mass at the Fatima shrine where he canonized Jacinta and Francisco Marto.

North Africa, South America, and India. With more than 10,000 members in 30 nations, the organization is now made up of separate yet linked branches: the Lay Marianist Communities, the Alliance Mariale, the Daughters of Mary Immaculate (the Marianist sisters), and the Society of Mary (the Marianist Brothers and Priests).

A more recent group is Our Lady's Rosary Makers, started in 1949 by Xaverian brother Sylvan Mattingly. He believed that he needed to do something for the Virgin and taught children and others how to make rosaries, which were then distributed to missions. He set up an office in Louisville, Kentucky, and named the group Our Lady of Fatima Rosary Making Club. Soon the group spread across the country, and it now produces more than 100,000 rosaries a year.

VISITATIONS AND SHRINES

Because of the belief in visitations by Mary, many fervently desire to visit the sites of her appearances. In 1917, Francisco and Jacinta Marto and their cousin, Lucia Dos Santos, encountered Mary while out herding sheep near their home in Fatima, Portugal. They saw the Virgin six times. Mary, they told others, brought with her a message for humankind. When word spread of what they saw, thousands flocked to Fatima to in the hope of experiencing her presence.

Francisco and Jacinta died soon after the sightings during the influenza epidemic at the end of World War I, he at age 10, she at nine. Lucia survived the plague that possibly killed more than 40 million people worldwide and became a Carmelite nun, living to 97. In 2008, three years after she died, the church began the process of her beatification, the first step toward canonization. Then, in May 2017, in front of a crowd of a hundred thousand pilgrims, Pope Francis canonized Francisco and Jacinta.

FATIMA'S THREE SECRETS

Along with her message of praying for others, Lucia revealed that Mary gave three apocalyptic secrets: The first foretold the coming of World War II; the second, the rise and collapse of communism. The third, which predicted the murder of a pope, was kept a secret by the Church, written down and kept in an envelope in the Vatican. When Mehmet Ali Ağca shot Pope John Paul II on May 13, 1981, during the

The Great Portal at the Cathedral of Santa Maria of Palma in Majorca

feast of Our Lady of Fatima, the pope believed "it was a mother's hand that guided the bullet's path" and saved his life. After he recovered, he asked to see the third Fatima secret, and read, "We saw . . . a Bishop dressed in white" who reminded the children of "the Holy Father . . . killed by group of soldiers who fired bullets and arrows at him."

John Paul became convinced of Lucia's visions and made pilgrimages to Fatima, donating one of the bullets that struck him to the shrine. It is kept in the crown of the statue of Mary. ∎

POPE JOHN PAUL II

Pope John Paul II was especially devoted to the Virgin Mary. When he was a student in Poland during World War II, he secretly made visits to pray before Our Lady of Czestochowa. This somber-looking icon is called the Black Madonna because it has become darkened by age. Poles lovingly call it the Queen of Poland and believe that it saved their land during the 17th-century battle of Czestochowa. John Paul so dearly cherished it that he had a replica of it hung over an altar at Castel Gandolfo, his papal retreat.

Pope John Paul II celebrated a Mass in Poland in 1995.

RELICS OF THE FAITHFUL

There is a long history of sacred relics, with churches displaying the bones, fingernails, and even heads of saints. But Mary was assumed into heaven and Jesus was resurrected, so there are no bodily remains for either. That has not stopped people from looking for and claiming to possess vials of Mary's mother's milk as well as Jesus' baby teeth and foreskin.

The trade in relics started in the Middle Ages when pilgrims making their way to the Holy Land returned with items they believed could help bring about miracles. Many proved to be fake. The 16th-century French theologian John Calvin commented on the extent of the trade when he noted, "If you were to collect all these pieces of the True Cross exhibited in various parts, they would form a whole cargo ship."

While there are forgeries, the church has determined some to be real. Many bear witness to the agonies of martyrs, such as the head of John the Baptist kept at Rome's Church of San Silvestro in Capite and a bone from a finger of the apostle Thomas at the nearby church of Santa Croce in Gerusalemme. For the faithful, they are deeply cherished as holy objects.

Relics associated with Jesus are the most sacred to Christians. The Cathedral of Notre Dame in Paris possesses the Crown of Thorns that Roman soldiers thrust on his head prior to the Crucifixion, though the cathedral's website notes that "its authenticity cannot be certified." A shroud said to have covered Jesus' body bears a haunting image of a man and is housed at Turin's Cathedral Santa Sindone. Scientific studies have all ascribed varying dates to it, but questions of authenticity have not stopped people from believing.

After relics associated with Jesus, the most highly prized are those related to Mary. People have sought out bits of her clothing and locks of her hair. The sixth-century historian Gregory of Tours wrote that relics of Jesus' mother were being revered, like a belt Mary handed to Thomas as she ascended to heaven. Called the *Sacra Cintola*, it made its way to Prato, Italy, in the 14th century. And a crypt below Rome's Santa Maria Maggiore contains a relic known as the Holy Crib, bits of ancient wood said to belong to the manger where Mary watched over her newborn baby.

Churches are filled with images and statues of Mary and other saints so that the faithful can take inspiration from them.

One place that holds special relevance to those seeking Mary is in the English county of Norfolk. In the 11th century, Richeldis de Faverches, a Saxon noblewoman in Walsingham, England, had three visions of Mary. During these moments, Jesus' mother transported her in spirit to Nazareth. There Mary showed Richeldis the spot where the angel told her that she would bear the child of God. She also instructed her to measure the home and construct it in England. Richeldis held a prayer vigil, and it is said that the house miraculously appeared whole in Walsingham. The town became known as England's Nazareth. It was a popular pilgrimage spot for the faithful to see Mary's home and gaze on a vial of her mother's milk. The path to the site became known as Pilgrims Way and was also called the Milky Way.

Two fiercely debated groups of Mary-related relics came to light in Jerusalem during the past four decades. One is an ossuary claimed to have contained the bones of one of Mary's other children. On its side is carved in Aramaic, "James son of Joseph brother of Jesus." The others come from a burial chamber where archaeologists discovered 10 ossuaries, one of which reads "Jesus son of Joseph" and others listing names that include Mary and Joseph. ∎

The Great Portal at the Cathedral of Santa Maria of Palma in Majorca

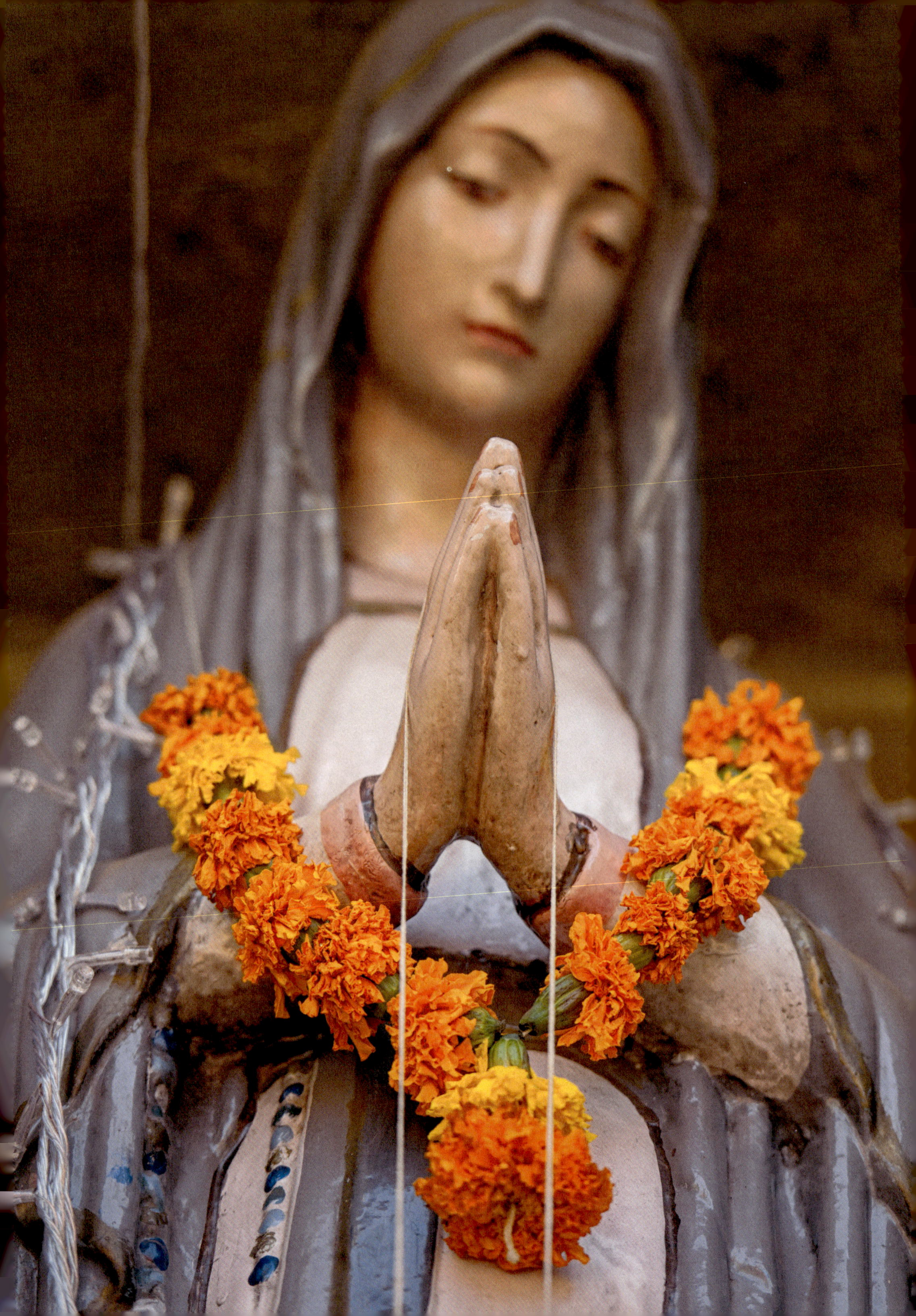

CHAPTER 5

EVER PRESENT

MARY IN OUR LIVES

Mary can seem omnipresent, appearing in paintings, literature, and music. Much of this is because people cherish her. They call to her, and when she responds, she often offers cryptic messages letting them know of upcoming events, warning of harm, and celebrating accomplishments.

And because she is all around us, many feel a need to protect her. This occurred in New York City in 1999. The Brooklyn Museum, which boasts such works as Lorenzo Monaco's 15th-century painting "Madonna of Humility' and Marco Palmezzano's 16th-century "Holy Family with Saints John the Baptist and Catherine of Alexandria," hosted "Sensation: Young British Artists from the Saatchi Collection." The exhibition contained pieces as shocking as a bust formed from nine pints of the artist's blood and a pig sliced in half, its carcass suspended in a tank filled with formaldehyde. When reporting on the upcoming opening, the New York *Daily News* headline screamed "B'klyn Gallery of Horror. Gruesome Museum Show Stirs Controversy."

None of the other works displayed, though, roiled the city like Chris Ofili's six-by-eight-foot painting "The Holy Virgin Mary." The image by the artist showing a black Mary smeared with elephant dung and dotted with clippings from pornographic magazines caused a furor. Mayor Rudolph Giuliani and others protested its inclusion in the show. The mayor not only called it anti-Catholic but threatened to cut off municipal funding. Not surprisingly, crowds showed up, and two months into its run, a retired schoolteacher who considered the painting "blasphemous" slipped past security and around a Plexiglas shield and spread white paint on the canvas. Museum staff had the painting cleaned and returned it to the show.

ABOVE: **A gold ring found in Tarsus, the place of St. Paul's birth.**
OPPOSITE: **A statue of the Virgin Mary decorated by supplicants with colorful garlands.**

THE STORY OF MARY

WORKS OF ART

——⦅∞⦆——

Mary's presence—her face, her words—has inspired countless people, making her one of the most familiar figures in the arts. She is presented as the patient mother, the caring friend, the grieving parent, the guiding light, the one who helps individuals and humanity. For the faithful, she is most importantly the one who helps those lost become found.

One who had lost his way was Dante Alighieri. The great 14th-century poet had spent years in exile, never returning to his beloved Florence. In his monumental work, *The Divine Comedy*, an embodiment of Dante takes a journey that can be seen as an allegory for his own life. Mary is his constant and largely unseen companion as he descends through the levels of hell, ascends into purgatory, and makes his way past the spheres of paradise.

THE JOURNEY TO MARY

Dante's narrative journey from the "dark wood" to the "celestial light," from earthly understanding to divine revelation, nears its end when he comes upon Mary. The poet wrote: "Virgin mother, daughter of your Son / Humbler and higher than all other creature . . . / You are she who so ennobled human nature / That nature's very maker did not disdain / To himself be made by you."

Mary is Dante's Mediatrix, the saint who lets him glimpse the omnipotent. And as with Dante's trek, there is a long history of artists seeking Mary. In 1723, a young Johann Sebastian Bach hoped to impress congregants in Leipzig and wrote a piece for Christmas vespers based on Luke's Magnificat. And Franz Schubert's created "Ave Maria! Hail Mary!" a musical prayer often remembered for Disney's interpretation in *Fantasia*.

SHRINES FOR THE FAITHFUL

By the fifth century, shrines and churches such as the one in Ephesus were being built to Mary. Cathedrals like the 14th-century Notre-Dame de Paris extol her and serve as a gathering place for her devoted. Filippo

---

THIS PAGE: **A 12th-century relief showing the Holy Family's flight to Egypt.** OPPOSITE: **A detail from a mosaic in Milan's Monumental Cemetery.**

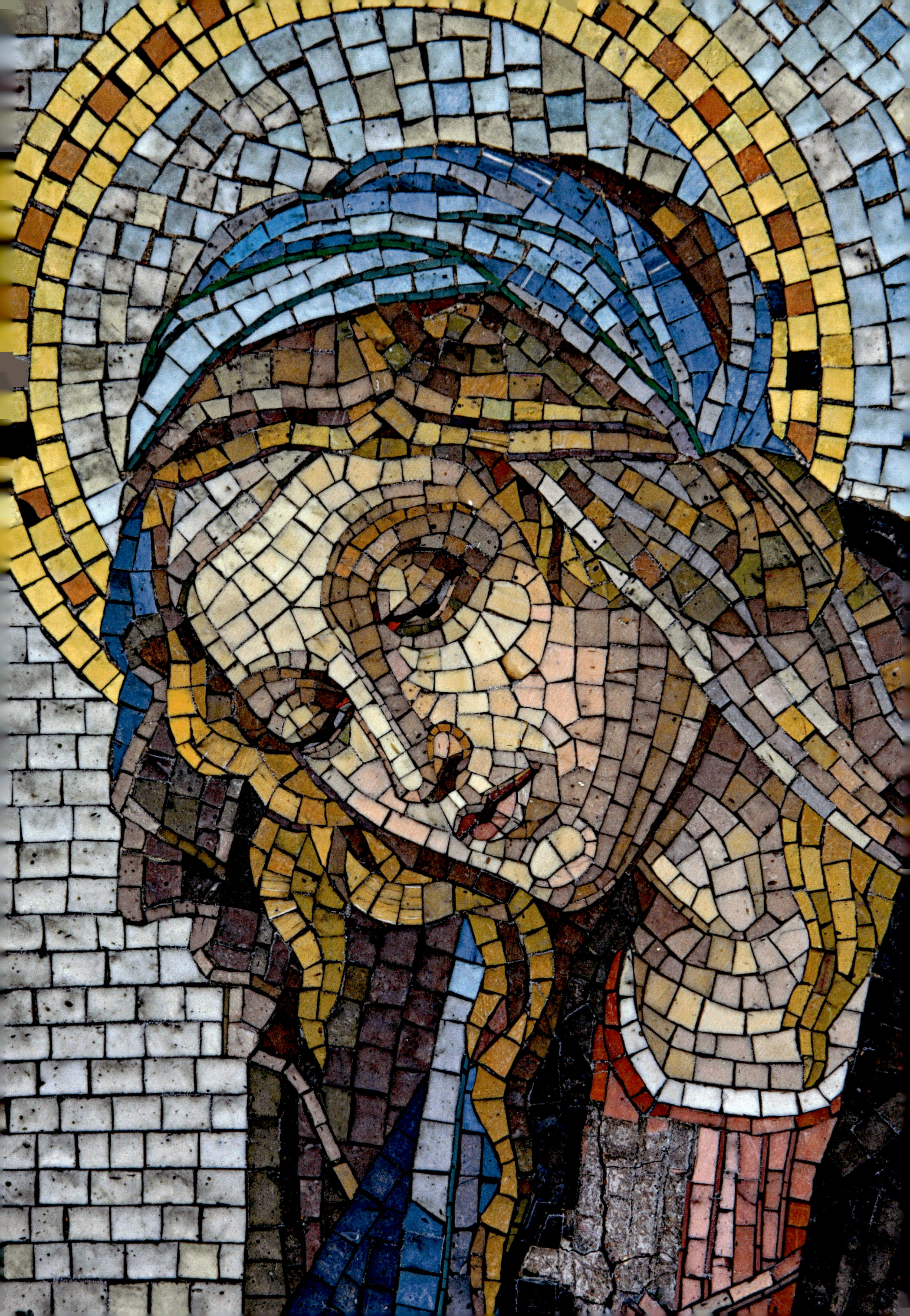

THE STORY OF MARY

"A MOSQUE IS NOW KNOWN AS MARY, MOTHER OF JESUS IN HOPES IT WILL CONSOLIDATE BONDS OF HUMANITY AMONG DIFFERENT RELIGIONS.

MICHELANGELO'S PIETÀS

According to tradition, Mary suffered seven sorrows, the sixth being her dead son's descent from the cross. Michelangelo was young when he first represented this scene in his "Pietà" for Rome's St. Peter's Basilica. The artist returned to the subject decades later. He planned "The Deposition" for his own tomb, showing Mary and others lowering Jesus from the cross, with Michelangelo's own face carved on the man assisting them. Before his death, Michelangelo started work on his "Pietà Rondanini," though he never completed the piece.

Michelangelo's "Pietà" at St. Peter's Basilica

Brunelleschi's 15th-century octagonal dome on Florence's Santa Maria del Fiore is the first such structure built without a supporting frame. It dominates the Florentine landscape and influenced such artists as Bramante. And in 2017, a mosque in the United Arab Emirates became known as Mary, Mother of Jesus, with Crown Prince Sheikh Mohammad bin Zayed Al-Nahyan hoping it would "consolidate bonds of humanity between followers of different religions."

It is in the visual arts, though—through painting, sculpture, and stained glass—where Mary is most recognized. Her visage is seen in infinitely varied portrayals that straddle the ages. Representations of Mary were rare in the early years of Christianity. There is a fresco of a woman with a baby in Rome's Catacombs of Santa Priscilla, which some believe is of Mary and Jesus. But after the church defined Mary as the Mother of God, she became central to art. Throughout Byzantium, her image appeared on icons hovering in churches below those of Christ and above the congregants, the motherly Mediatrix ready to intercede between humanity and God.

A MORE GLORIOUS MARY

When devotional portraits of Mary spread across western Europe during the Middle Ages, they tapped images similar to those in Byzantium. But as the Renaissance approached and the rigidity of medieval art gave way to a vibrant realism, Mary appeared as both more approachable—such as a peasant with a golden filigreed halo hovering around her head—and glorious, as the ruling Queen of Heaven floating in the firmament, surrounded by attentive angels.

That age exploded with works about her, as with a young Raphael's 1504 "Marriage of the Virgin," where the artist rendered the ideal virgin in the midst of classical splendor. And there is Michelangelo's iridescent "Doni Tondo," a sculptural-looking canvas of the Holy Family. It wasn't just in Catholic countries where Mary appeared. In Holland, a nation not known for its imagery of saints and apostles, Rembrandt van Rijn painted a series of biblical portraits at the end of his life, including his mournful "The Virgin of Sorrows." ∎

A stained glass window of Mary and her newborn at St. Mary's Church in New Trier, Minnesota

THE STORY OF MARY

The Many Faces of Mary

Mary hailed from the tribe of Judah and would have had a Mediterranean complexion with dark hair and eyes. Yet as Christianity grew, it spread beyond Israel. Artists as far afield as the Netherlands, Argentina, and Korea have embraced her as one of their own, sketching her likeness on paper, painting her on canvas, molding her in glass, and carving her from stone. All the while, they have sought to define her love in order to inspire those around them.

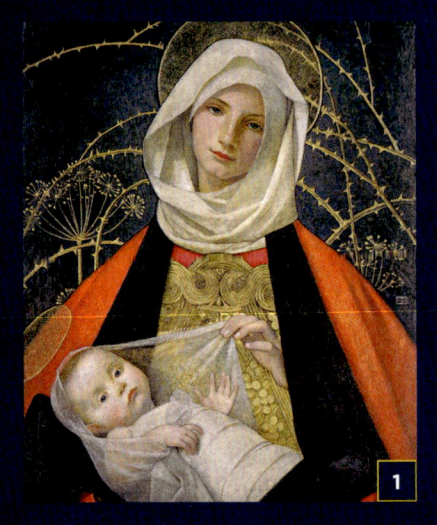

1 | ENGLAND
Marianne Stokes's painting at the Wolverhampton Art Gallery of an angelic-looking Madonna cradling her newborn child

2 | ARGENTINA
A stained glass window at the Basilica of Our Lady of Luján. Our Lady of Luján is considered the patroness of Argentina, Paraguay, and Uruguay.

3 | ETHIOPIA
An 18th-century painting on cloth of Mary and Jesus at the Addis Ababa Museum

4 | ISRAEL
A Chinese tile painting in the Church of the Annunciation in Nazareth

5 | SPAIN
The black Madonna at the Royal Monastery of Santa María de Guadalupe

6 | UNITED STATES
A contemporary portrait of Mary and Jesus by the Haitian-born American artist Patricia Brintle is a vibrant representation of them.

7 | GREECE
A Greek Orthodox icon from Thessaloniki, Greece, depicting the Virgin Mary and a young yet infinitely wise-looking Jesus

98

EVER PRESENT

THE STORY OF MARY

SACRED SITES

As the Mediatrix, Mary has appeared to people over the centuries. There are many, many claims of visitations by her. Quite a few have drawn attention, and a number of locales attract both pilgrims in the need of guidance and supplicants navigating both the corporeal and the temporal as they fervently pray for a personal encounter with the Mother of God.

One day in 1531, Juan Diego was rushing to Mass for the Feast of the Immaculate Conception near Mexico City, Mexico. As he did, he came upon a glowing woman who spoke to him in Nahuatl, his native language. "I wish that a temple be erected here quickly, so I may therein exhibit and give all my love, compassion, help, and protection," she reportedly instructed the Christian convert. Diego told the bishop what he experienced, but the cleric did not believe him. When Mary returned, she instructed Diego to gather flowers. Even though it was winter, he found roses, and as he opened his cloak to hand them to the bishop, Mary's image miraculously appeared emblazoned on his clothes. Twenty million people a year visit the Mexico City basilica to see the Our Lady of the Guadalupe icon reportedly from Diego's cloak and attend one of the hourly masses.

LOURDES

Probably the most famous pilgrimage site is Lourdes in France. In 1858, 14-year-old Marie-Bernarde "Bernadette" Soubirous was heading to the nearby Massabielle grotto when she saw a shimmering woman who told her, "I am the Immaculate Conception." The woman is believed to have spoken to Bernadette of helping the poor, of love, of penance, saying, "Tell the priests to build a chapel here." The community cleaned the grotto, which had served as a garbage dump. Word spread of the visitation, and now six million people visit Lourdes every year. The sick seeking relief take part in the Procession of the Blessed Sacrament and drink the grotto's spring water, which is believed to have curative powers.

AMERICA'S VISION

In 1859, a year after Mary showed herself to Bernadette, Adele Brise, an immigrant from Dion-le-Val, Belgium,

---

THIS PAGE: **A delicate glass-blown vase from the Holy Land from around 50 B.C.E.** OPPOSITE: **Pope John Paul II followed a statue of the Virgin of Fatima in Portugal before celebrating a Mass in 1991.**

100

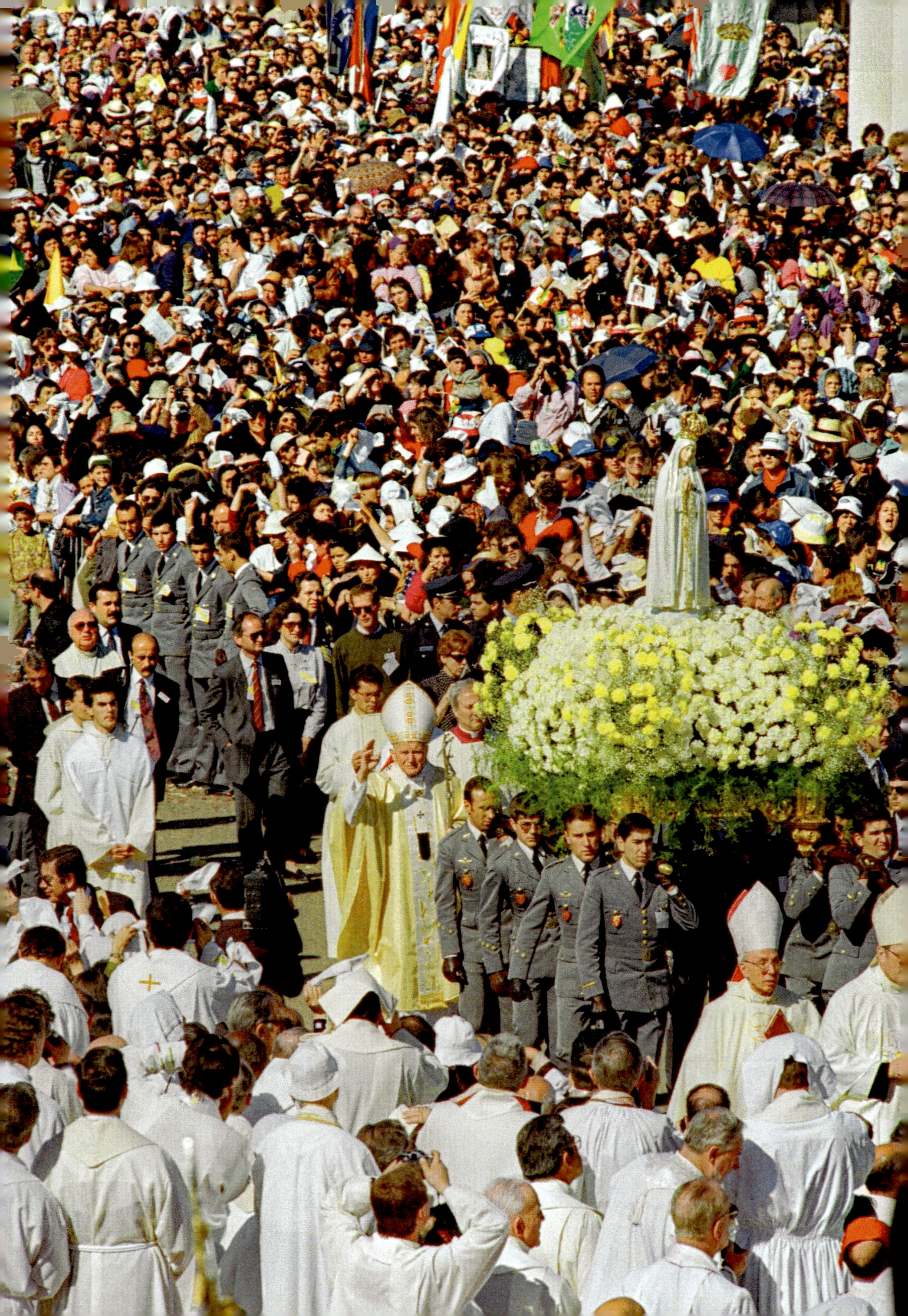

THE STORY OF MARY

People lighting candles at the Deir al Adra monastery in Minya, Egypt

saw Mary as she floated in the air between two trees in Champion, Wisconsin. The virgin was dressed in white, and above her head sat a crown made of stars. "I am the Queen of Heaven who prays for the conversion of sinners," she told Brise. Mary visited her three times and instructed her, "Gather the children in this wild country and teach them what they should know for salvation." Fulfilling Mary's command, Brise spent the rest of her life teaching Catholicism to children. In 2010, the site on which Our Lady of Good Hope shrine now stands became the first locale in the United States to have a church-validated apparition of the Virgin.

GENOCIDE FORETOLD

On November 28, 1981, Alphonsine Mumureke stood in the dining room at her school run by nuns in Kibeho, Rwanda, when she heard a voice call out, "My daughter." The 16-year-old Mumureke asked who spoke to her and the voice said, "I am the Mother of the Word." The visitor said she came because she heard the girl's prayers. Over the next eight years, Mary appeared not only to Mumureke but also to two other young students there: Nathalie Mukamazimpaka and Marie Claire Mukangango. Among other things,

MARY'S TOMB

In the 12th century, the Crusaders built the Church of the Assumption, also known as Church of the Dormition, in Jerusalem. The basilica with its circular staircase leads down to a burial space carved out of rock. Like Jesus' tomb at the nearby Chapel of the Ascension, Mary's grave is empty, for she rose toward heaven, either as Catholics maintain while she lived or as Orthodox contend when her heavenly sleep began. The Greek, Armenian, Syriac, Coptic, and Ethiopian Orthodox churches share rights over the space.

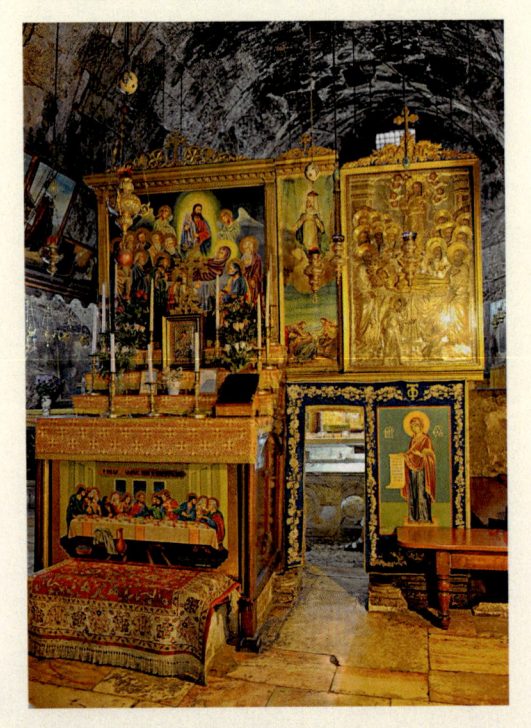

Mary's tomb in Jerusalem

Many gather at Lourdes's Massabielle grotto, where Mary first spoke to Marie-Bernarde "Bernadette" Soubirous in 1858.

the Virgin warned of a coming genocide, of "rivers of blood" washing over their land. Her words proved tragically true. In 1994, Rwanda's Hutu majority slaughtered 800,000 of their Tutsi neighbors, including Mukangango. Seven years later, the Vatican declared the apparitions valid, and today Kibeho's Shrine of Our Lady of Sorrows draws people to southern Rwanda from throughout Africa and the world.

BELIEF BEYOND PROOF

The same year that Mary first approached Mumureke, six children—Mirjana Dragicevic, Ivanka Ivankovic, Vicka Ivankovic, Ivan Dragicevic, Marija Pavlovic, and

> THE **VIRGIN** WARNED OF A COMING **GENOCIDE**, OF **"RIVERS OF BLOOD"** ENGULFING THEIR LAND OF RWANDA. HER WORDS PROVED TRAGICALLY **TRUE.**

Jakov Colo—in Medjugorje in the Bosnian mountains claimed to have seen Mary. And while a 1991 commission could not establish that the supernatural had manifested itself, it hasn't stopped people from flocking to Medjugorje. So far, 40 million people have journeyed there, and a few of the now grown children post their newest visions online. ∎

103

FEAST DAYS AND CELEBRATIONS

The church celebrates days throughout the year with solemnities, memorials, and feasts. Solemnities are the most important days—such as Sunday, Easter, and Christmas—and relate to Christ and important saints. Feasts are considered just below solemnities on the liturgical calendar, and memorials are the lowest ranks of the days.

There are many days associated with Mary found in various churches. The Catholic Church starts with the Solemnity of Mary on January 1 and has set aside such celebrations as the May 31 Visitation of the Blessed Virgin Mary Feast and the December 8 Feast of the Immaculate Conception. The Eastern Orthodox Church marks the annunciation on March 25 and the Feast of Mary's Birth on September 8. The Ethiopian Orthodox Church has the January 1 Feast of Mary, Mother of God. The Coptic Church on June 1 celebrates the Escape of the Holy Family to Egypt. The Anglican Communion observes July 26 for Parents of the Blessed Virgin Mary, and the Lutherans also observe Marian feast days.

GLOBAL CELEBRATIONS

An annual feast for Mary occurred as early as 625 in the Holy Land. In the Middle Ages, there were annunciation pageants. In Germany a boy was dressed as an angel and lowered from an opening in the church's ceiling called the "Holy Ghost Hole." In Russia, the priests blessed wafers and congregants planted crumbs of this Annunciation bread to protect crops.

In Wales, February's Feast of the Purification of the Virgin marks when Mary and Joseph presented the newborn Jesus at the Temple. To celebrate, townspeople walk around their communities and sing carols. In Poland, legend has it that on that day, Mary would visit villages and scare away wolves.

Thousands of family members pray the rosary in Montevideo, Uruguay, in 2017.

A Holy Mass at a Marian shrine in La Salette, France

THE FEAST OF THE ASSUMPTION

Catholics celebrate the August 15 Feast of the Assumption. In Hungary, tradition holds that its first king, St. Stephen, crowned the Virgin as that nation's patroness. In France, priests bless fields of corn, and in Armenia, they bless the grapes. In Portugal, boats earn a special blessing. The tradition made its way to communities like Provincetown, Massachusetts, where a priest blesses vessels as parishioners dance. In Ireland and Great Britain, the faithful take dips in lakes, rivers, and the ocean.

GOD'S OTHER CREATURES

Since the early 18th century, European cat snakes have appeared at the monastery on the island of Kefalonia in the Ionian Sea during the Orthodox Feast of the Dormition of the Theotokos. According to legend, nuns prayed to Mary when they were about to be attacked by pirates; the snakes massed and scared away the dreaded marauders. Ever since, the snakes arrive during the August feast and parishioners carry them into the church to touch the silver icon known as the Panagia Fidoussa, or the Virgin of the Snakes.

Each September 8, Indian Catholic migrants in Israel celebrate the Nativity of Mary. In Jaffa, congregants march in traditional attire and sing, then attend a Mass held in their native language.

Latin America has grand celebrations. December 12 is the feast day of Our Lady of Guadalupe. Celebrants accompanied by bands descend on Mexico City, carrying banners and images of Mary and dancing and singing *mañanitas,* a traditional birthday song to her. ∎

THE STORY OF MARY

SIGHTINGS PAST AND PRESENT

Appearances of Mary began in 40 C.E. when St. James the Greater saw Mary in Spain. The church began investigating such visions in the 16th century. They have since spread, and some claim that there have been 2,500 sightings throughout history and 500 in the 20th century. Despite this, the Catholic, Episcopalian, Coptic, and other churches have approved only a handful.

The most famous and recognized are in Guadalupe, Mexico, in 1531; Rue du Bac, France, in 1830; Lourdes in 1858; and Fatima in 1917. Some take years to earn a religious imprimatur. In the early 1660s, Benôite Rencurel, a young girl from Saint-Étienne d'Avançon, France, was tending her neighbor's sheep when she saw Mary holding a child. Benôite offered to share her bread with the woman and asked to hold the baby. The Virgin smiled and returned each day to talk to Benôite. Mary asked that a chapel be built in Laus along with a home for a priest. It soon was, and when Benôite grew up, she became a lay Dominican. She received visions of the Virgin until her death in 1718. Mary's appearance was recognized by the church in 2008, and the shrine of Our Lady of Laus attracts 120,000 pilgrims each year; numerous healings have been associated with the site.

VISIONS OF MARY AND JOSEPH

In August 1879, Mary McLoughlin, a housekeeper for the archdeacon of Knock, Ireland, said she saw "a wonderful number of strange figures; one like the blessed Virgin Mary and one like St. Joseph," on the side of the town's parish church. And though it rained heavily, the water did not fall on the vision. McLoughlin told others, and 14 townspeople came out and witnessed the same miraculous vision. Mary Byrne, who stood in the rain for more than an hour to watch Mary, recalled, "She wore a crown on the head, rather a large crown, and it appeared to me somewhat yellower than the dress or robes worn by Our Blessed Lady. In the figure of St. Joseph the head was slightly bent, and inclined towards the Blessed Virgin, as if paying her respect. It represented the saint as somewhat aged, with grey whiskers and greyish hair."

A GOLDEN ROSE

Two months later, the witnesses testified before a Commission of Enquiry, which found their statements both trustworthy

Combs like this dating from the time of the Roman occupation have been found at numerous Judean sites.

" IN 2015, PARISHIONERS RECITING THE LORD'S PRAYER AT SYDNEY'S ST. CHARBEL'S CHURCH SAW THE LIPS ON A PAINTING OF THE VIRGIN MOVE.

and satisfactory. As word spread, people arrived, and the archdeacon had to handle many extra daily masses and confessions. In 1936, a church investigative commission accepted their vision. And then on the 100th anniversary of the visitations, more than 450,000 people descended on tiny Knock to greet Pope John Paul II, who presented the shrine with a Golden Rose, a pure gold ornament that is an important sign of papal honor.

Some recent sightings have not only attracted the faithful, but also the curious and the news media. In 2003, people started flocking to Coogee Beach near Sydney, Australia, where sunlight reflecting off a fence appeared to reveal a veiled figure. People who came to see it sang and wept. In July 2015, parishioners reciting the Lord's Prayer at Sydney's St. Charbel's Church saw the lips on a painting of the Virgin move.

Pilgrims making their way to Mexico City's Basilica of Our Lady of Guadalupe to celebrate Mary's 1531 appearance to Juan Diego

THE STORY OF MARY

THIS PAGE: **Two young girls in West Chicago, Illinois, look at a tree trunk that some say bears an image of the Virgin Mary.** OPPOSITE: **Pilgrims in 2016 gathered in La Vang, Vietnam, where Mary appeared in 1798.**

A STATUE TRANSFORMS

Later in 2015, congregants at the Church of St. Thomas More in Subang Jaya, Malaysia, reported that a statue of the Virgin, Our Lady of Fatima, not only appeared alive, but grew, smiled, cried, and seemed to turn from fiberglass to porcelain. According to a parishioner, "Her eyes were moving very slowly; all of us were there and we saw it. The father was saying, 'Look at her, she's looking at us. She was full of life; she had a lot of tears in her eyes.' When we started singing 'Ave Maria,' she started smiling and her lips were moving."

Others see Mary in more unexpected spaces, such as during a meal. In the early 1990s, Diana Duyser took a bite of her grilled cheese sandwich and noticed the Virgin Mary's image on the food. The Florida woman placed the sandwich along with cotton balls into a clear plastic box and set it on her nightstand. According to Duyser, it never sprouted mold. After she offered it on eBay in 2004, the online casino GoldenPalace.com paid $28,000 for it. The firm's CEO, Richard Rowe, said he was going to use it to raise money for charity.

THE EYE OF THE BELIEVER

While the faithful adhere to their belief, scientists have described the perception of people's faces in inanimate objects as "face pareidolia." As the brain develops, it learns to recognize faces, and it can start to identify and perceive faces on unrelated objects with only a minor resemblance to people. The journal *Cortex* noted in a press release for its article "Seeing Jesus in Toast," that "Instead of the phrase 'seeing is believing,' the results suggest that 'believing is seeing.'" ∎

Ave Maria

ĐỨC MẸ HIỆN RA TẠI ĐÂY 1798

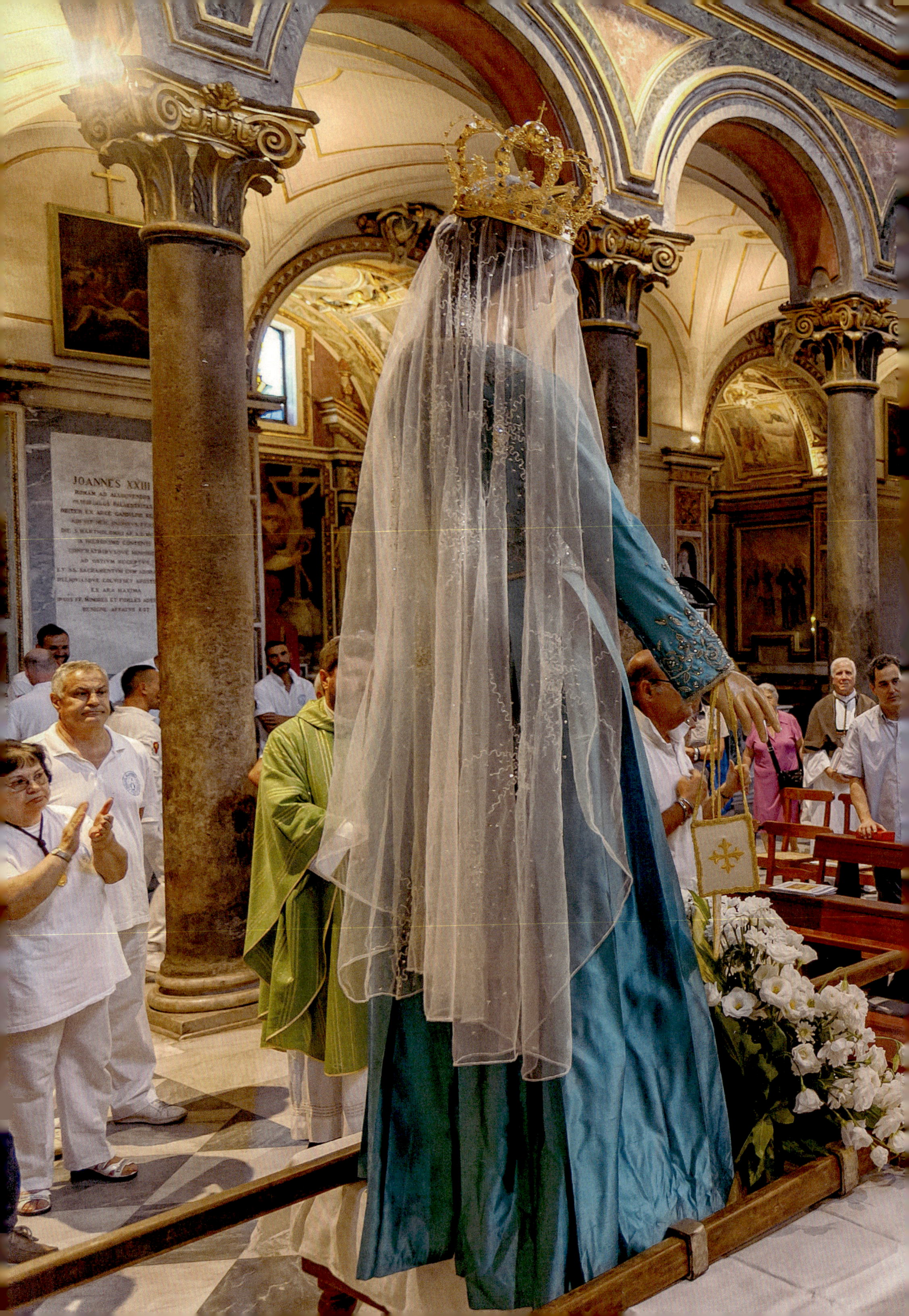
JOANNES XXIII

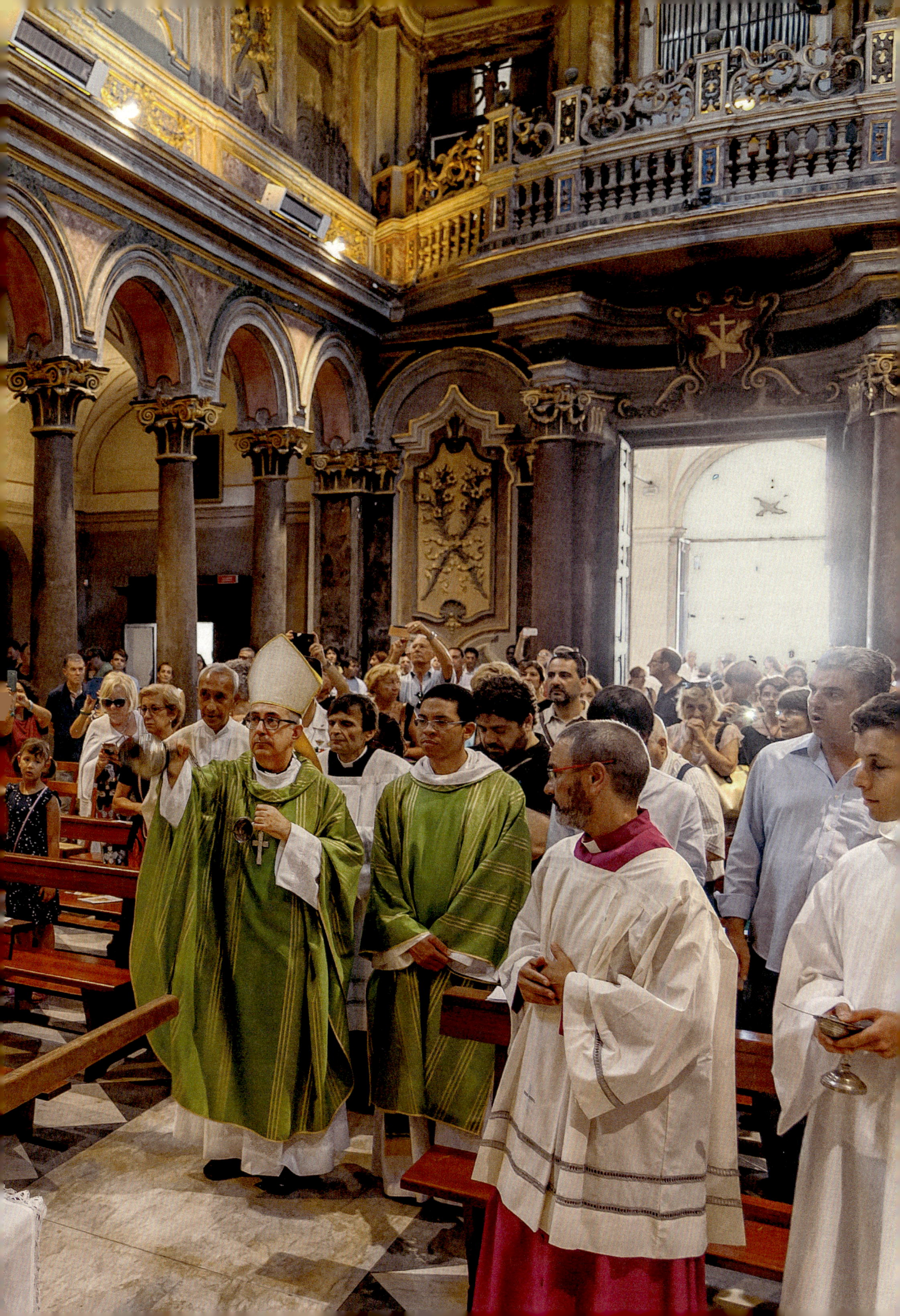

The Story of Mary

Daniel S. Levy

PRODUCED BY NATIONAL GEOGRAPHIC PARTNERS, LLC
1145 17th Street NW
Washington, DC 20036-4688 USA

Copyright © 2018 National Geographic Partners, LLC.
All rights reserved.

NATIONAL GEOGRAPHIC and Yellow Border Design
are trademarks of the National Geographic Society, used
under license.

ISSN 2160-7141

Printed and distributed by Time Inc. Books
225 Liberty Street
New York, NY 10281

Printed in the USA

Grateful acknowledgment is made to:
New American Bible, revised edition
Shaye J. D. Cohen, Harvard University
Byron McCane, Florida Atlantic University
Carol Meyers, Duke University
Elaine Pagels, Princeton University
Joseph Pierro
Miri Rubin, Queen Mary University of London
Stephen Shoemaker, University of Oregon

ILLUSTRATIONS CREDITS

Cover, Sassoferrato, Il (Giovanni Battista Salvi) (1609-1685)/Palazzo Ducale, Urbino, Italy/Bridgeman Images; 0-1, Diana Markosian; 3, Guido Reni/Getty; 4, Buonarroti, Michelangelo (1475-1564)/St. Peter's, Vatican City/Bridgeman Images; 6, Lippi, Filippo (ca 1406-1469) (and workshop)/Corsham Court, Wiltshire/Bridgeman Images; 7, Diana Markosian; 10, Adolfo Bezzi/Electa/Mondadori Portfolio via Getty; 11, Pantheon Studios, Inc.; 12, Pantheon Studios, Inc.; 13, Alfredo Dagli Orti/REX/Shutterstock; 15, Raphael (Raffaello Sanzio of Urbino) (1483-1520)/Pinacoteca di Brera, Milan, Italy/Bridgeman Images; 16, Tour, Georges de la (1593-1652)/Musée des Beaux-Arts, Nantes, France/Bridgeman Images; 16-17, Ira Block/NG Creative; 18, Pantheon Studios, Inc.; 19 (UP), Pantheon Studios, Inc.; 19 (LO), Chris Anderson; 20, Pantheon Studios, Inc.; 21, Giotto di Bondone (ca 1266-1337)/San Francesco, Lower Church, Assisi, Italy/Bridgeman Images; 22-3, Botticelli, Sandro (Alessandro di Mariano di Vanni Filipepi) (1444/5-1510)/National Gallery of Art, Washington DC, USA/Bridgeman Images; 23, Pantheon Studios, Inc.; 24, The Israel Museum, Jerusalem, Israel/Bridgeman Images; 25, Protasov AN/Shutterstock.com; 26, DeAgostini/DEA Picture Library/Getty; 27 (UP), Rohden, Franz von (1817-1903)/Allen Memorial Art Museum, Oberlin College, Ohio, USA/Mrs. F. F. Prentiss Fund/Bridgeman Images; 27 (LO), Dr. Ken Dark; 28, Michael Melford/NG Creative; 29, Pantheon Studios, Inc.; 31, Pantheon Studios, Inc.; 32, Cosimo, Piero di (ca 1462-1521)/Palazzo Barberini, Gallerie Nazionali Barberini Corsini, Rome, Italy/Bridgeman Images; 32-3, Pantheon Studios, Inc.; 34, Richard T. Nowitz/Corbis via Getty; 35 (UP), Pantheon Studios, Inc.; 35 (LO), ChameleonsEye/Shutterstock.com; 36, Pinacoteca Capitolina, Palazzo Conservatori, Rome, Italy/Bridgeman Images; 37, Raphael (Raffaello Sanzio of Urbino) (1483-1520)/Vatican Museums and Galleries, Vatican City/Bridgeman Images; 38, ChameleonsEye/Shutterstock.com; 42, Universal History Archive/UIG/REX/Shutterstock; 43, Michael Melford/NG Creative; 45, Copping, Harold (1863-1932)/Private Collection/© Look and Learn/Bridgeman Images; 46, Francken, Frans the Elder (1542-1616)/Musee Municipal, Dunkirk, France/Bridgeman Images; 47 (UP), © Balage Balogh/Art Resource, NY; 47 (LO), Pantheon Studios, Inc.; 48, Gianni Dagli Orti/REX/Shutterstock; 49, Pantheon Studios, Inc.; 50, Pantheon Studios, Inc.; 51, DEA/A. Dagli Orti/Getty; 52, Gianni Dagli Orti/REX/Shutterstock; 54, The Israel Museum, Jerusalem, Israel/Gift of Jack and Jane Weprin/Bridgeman Images; 55, Pantheon Studios, Inc.; 57, Gianni Dagli Orti/REX/Shutterstock; 58, Mike Nelson/EPA/REX/Shutterstock; 58-9, Photo Josse/Leemage/Corbis via Getty; 60, Philippe Lissac/Getty; 61 (UP), Pantheon Studios, Inc.; 61 (LO), Kenneth Garrett/NG Creative; 62, Pantheon Studios, Inc.; 63, Gianni Dagli Orti/REX/Shutterstock; 64 (UP), Godong/robertharding/Getty; 64 (LO), Izzet Keribar/Lonely Planet Images/Getty; 65, Sezai Sahmay/Shutterstock; 66, Pantheon Studios, Inc.; 67, DEA/A. De Gregorio/Getty; 68, DeAgostini/Getty; 69, R. Classen/Shutterstock; 70, Raphael/Getty; 71, Pantheon Studios, Inc.; 72, National Maritime Museum, Haifa, Israel/Erich Lessing/Art Resource, NY; 73, Imagno/Getty; 74, Badisches Landesmuseum, Karlsruhe, Germany/Bridgeman Images; 75, The Art Archive/REX/Shutterstock; 76, Philippe Lissac/Getty; 77, Fabriano, Gentile da (ca 1370-1427)/Galleria degli Uffizi, Florence, Tuscany, Italy/Bridgeman Images; 78, Pantheon Studios, Inc.; 79, Attributed to Francesco Solimena (1657-1747), Cathedral of San Pardo, Larino, Molise, Italy, 18th century/De Agostini Picture Library/A. De Gregorio/Bridgeman Images; 80, Pantheon Studios, Inc.; 81, Titian (Tiziano Vecellio) (ca 1488-1576)/Santa Maria Gloriosa dei Frari, Venice, Italy/Cameraphoto Arte Venezia/Bridgeman Images; 82, Correggio (Antonio Allegri) (ca 1489-1534)/Duomo of Parma, Italy/Alinari/Bridgeman Images; 83, Claudio Giovanni Colombo/Shutterstock; 85, Pablo Blazquez Dominguez/Getty; 86, Sergey Ryzhkov/Shutterstock; 86-7, mauritius images GmbH/Alamy; 88, Pedro Fiúza/NurPhoto via Getty; 89 (UP), Manuel Cohen/Art Resource, NY; 89 (LO), Franco Origlia/Getty; 90, GOLFX/Shutterstock; 91, Renata Sedmakova/Shutterstock.com; 92, Design Pics Inc./NG Creative; 93, Pantheon Studios, Inc.; 94, Private Collection/Joanna Booth/Bridgeman Images; 95, Godong/Robert Harding Picture Library; 96, Nancy Bauer/Shutterstock.com; 97, S.Tatiana/Shutterstock.com; 98 (UP LE), Stokes, Marianne (1855-1927)/Wolverhampton Art Gallery, West Midlands, UK/Bridgeman Images; 98 (LO LE), Martin Gray/NG Creative; 98 (RT), Werner Forman Archive/Bridgeman Images; 99 (UP LE), Ryan Rodrick Beiler/Alamy; 99 (UP RT), Monasterio Real, Guadalupe, Spain/Bridgeman Images; 99 (LO LE), Brintle, Patricia/Private Collection/Bridgeman Images; 99 (LO RT), Godong/Robert Harding Picture Library; 100, Pantheon Studios, Inc.; 101, Derrick Ceyrac/AFP/Getty; 102 (UP), Diana Markosian; 102 (LO), Vladimir Blinov/Alamy; 103, Christophe Ena/AP/REX/Shutterstock; 104, Carlos Lebrato/Anadolu Agency/Getty; 105, Pascal Deloche/GODONG/Getty; 106, Pantheon Studios, Inc.; 107, Rick Gerharter/Lonely Planet Images/Getty; 108, Stephen J. Carrera/AP/REX/Shutterstock; 109, Hong Hanh Mac Thi/Alamy Stock Photo; 110-111, Stefano Montesi/Corbis via Getty; 113, Gentileschi, Orazio (1563-1639) (after)/© Purix Verlag Volker Christen/Bridgeman Images.

PREVIOUS PAGES: **Monsignor Gianrico Ruzza blesses the Madonna Fiumarola as part of Rome's 2017 Festa de' Noantri.**
OPPOSITE: **"The Annunciation" by Italian baroque painter Orazio Gentileschi.**

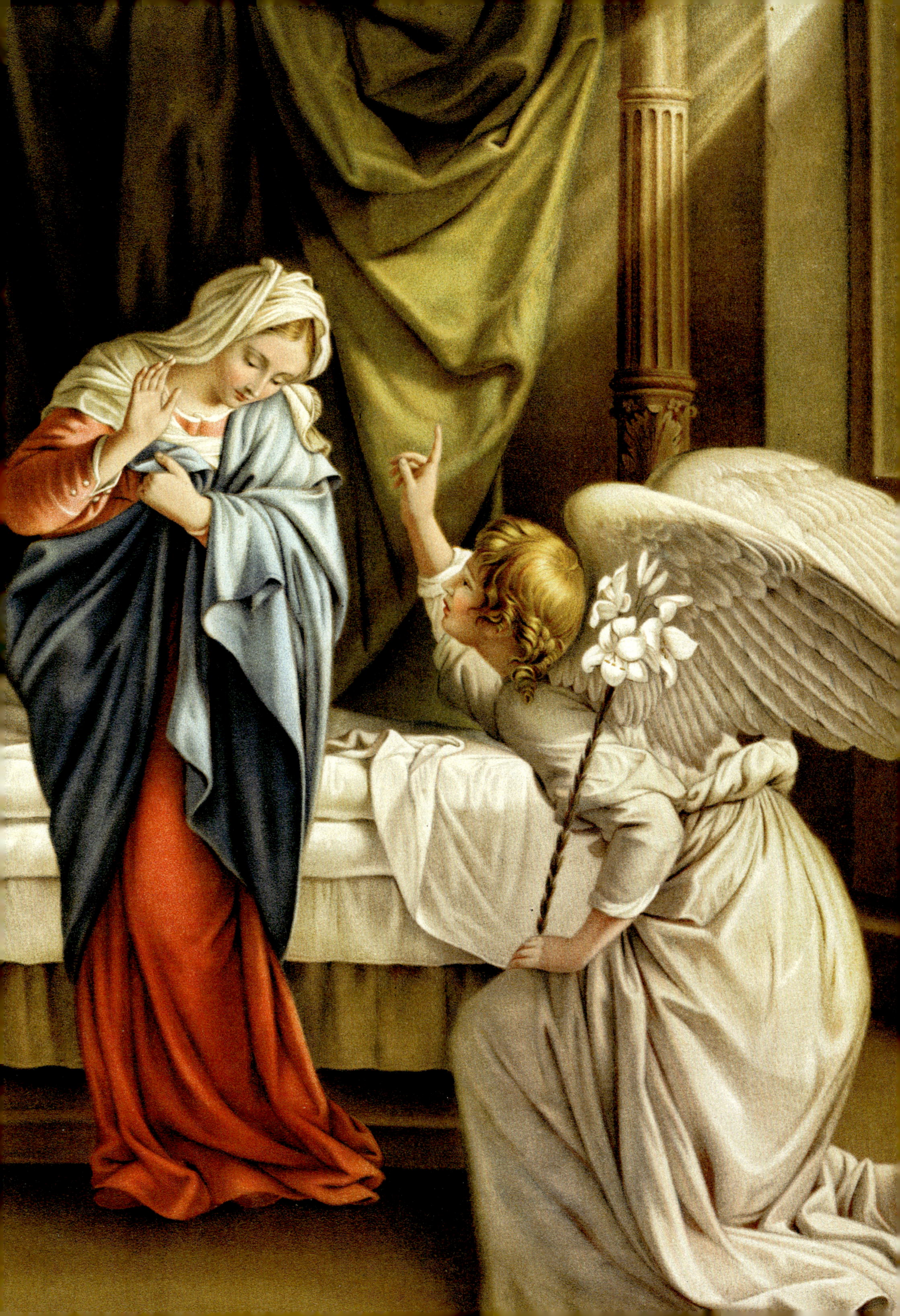

Made in the USA
Middletown, DE
04 May 2018